THE BROWN PLAGUE

THE BROWN PLAGUE

PLAGUE

TRAVELS IN LATE WEIMAR

& EARLY NAZI GERMANY

by Daniel Guérin

Translated and with an introduction by

Robert Schwartzwald

■

Duke University Press   *Durham and London 1994*

© 1994 Duke University Press
All rights reserved
Printed in the United States of America
on acid-free paper ∞
Library of Congress
Cataloging-in-Publication data
appear on the last page of this book.
Typeset in Adobe Garamond by
Keystone Typesetting, Inc.

To Daniel Guérin,
who was happy to know that
La Peste brune would finally be
available in English.

CONTENTS

ACKNOWLEDGMENTS

This translation and its accompanying documentation would not have
been possible without the help of many people and institutions. Sean
Holland was an astute reader of the introductory essay as it took final
form, generously interweaving emotional and intellectual nourishment.
Bruce Russell spent long hours going over the Introduction and the trans-
lation and offered many valuable suggestions. Paul Peters and Rosemary
Hnatiuk helped with German terms and song lyrics. Klaus Mayr in Linz,
Austria, found and summarized the article by Christine Fournier on the
Ringvereine, and my colleague Thomas Cassirer's recollections of Weimar
Berlin resonate in his translation of it. Anne Clarken typed earlier versions
of the manuscript. Archivists at the Bibliothèque de documentation internationale contemporaine at the Université de Paris–Nanterre facilitated
my examination of the papers and documents Daniel Guérin had depos-
ited there; Jean Le Bitoux and Jacques Vandemborghe of M-Com/Fonda-
tion Mémoire des sexualités in Paris provided access to letters and photos
that Daniel Guérin confided to them upon his death. Professor Michel
Trébitsch of Paris took the time to meet and answer my many questions
about the political and social conjuncture in France in the 1930s and
provided information on the character of the newspapers for which Guérin
wrote. The University of Massachusetts at Amherst provided important
Educational Needs funding at crucial stages of this project.

   In preparing the translation, I had the opportunity to meet with Daniel
Guérin on several occasions, and I will always be grateful for his generosity
in providing me with documents and photographs from his personal collection. Most of all I will cherish his recollections, analytical and anecdotal,

■

of a long and extraordinary life as related in his Paris apartment and especially against the backdrop of the beach and the factories of La Ciotat. For La Ciotat is not only a Mediterranean town set beneath a stunning *corniche,* but as one might expect of Daniel Guérin's choice for a home in the Midi, it is an industrial working-class center as well!

INTRODUCTION

Robert Schwartzwald

L*a Peste brune* (*The Brown Plague*) is Daniel Guérin's eyewitness account of the fall of the Weimar Republic and the first months of the Third Reich. It is based on two tours he took through Germany in 1932 and 1933, immediately before and after Hitler's appointment as chancellor. When Guérin initially prepared his testimony for publication, his aim was not only to warn French workers of the horrors of fascism but to publicize the resistance to it inside Germany. Even though these accounts of resistance may appear exaggerated or overly optimistic in retrospect, they fill a gap in our appreciation of this turbulent period and remind us that in the early 1930s, there was nothing inevitable about the consolidation of Nazism. In so doing, the text underscores the tragedy of fascism's victory.

Guérin toured Germany first on foot and then on bicycle, traveling from youth hostel to hostel. In this way he came into contact with the thousands of German youths who found relief from the economic crisis by journeying from one town to the next and resting in each hostel for the permitted time. As he crisscrossed the country, it did not take Guérin long to appreciate the seductive energies of Nazism. In *The Brown Plague,* he brings into relief its ability to exploit a yearning for change through the skilled use of spectacle, costume, and ritual that appeal to subconscious structures of desire and eroticism. At the same time, Guérin chronicles the collapse of the German workers' movement, then considered the mightiest in non-Soviet Europe. Through blow-by-blow depictions and vivid dialogue, he offers poignant insights into the unfolding tragedy. As a result, *The Brown Plague*'s account of the fateful months surrounding the Nazis' seizure of power differs in style and focus from standard political histories and should particularly interest readers for whom an appreciation of this major political defeat of the twentieth century is inseparable from an understanding of the sexual and cultural politics of fascism.

In the course of his visits to Germany, Guérin not only observes Nazi festivals, youth activities, and party rallies in village and city alike, but also recounts the growing stridency of anti-Semitism and the ghoulish ambiance of a book burning. Guérin despairs after touring the opulent People's House in Dresden, at once so magnificent and so fragile in its isolation from the very class it is supposed to serve, but he is heartened by a visit to Kuhle Wampe, the proletarian lakeside tent city near Berlin made famous by Slatan Dudow and Bertolt Brecht's documentary film. Guérin's accounts of the destructive quarrels among Communist and Social Democratic leaders despite the efforts of rank-and-file members to unite against fascism are followed by reports from centers of clandestine resistance and from the working-class neighborhoods and factories that were being brutalized into submission. By observing a crucial session of the Reichstag presided over by Hermann Göring, Guérin is able to take the measure of the different parliamentary parties in action; by staying in the youth hostels, he hears firsthand what young Communists and Socialists, and, of course, the Hitler Youth, have to say about Germany's future. Finally, Guérin discovers the *Wild-clique,* gangs of youths living in the forests who have assumed the names and composite costumes of Wild West cowboys and Indians, Teutonic knights, and pirates celebrated in escapist and exoticist popular novels of the time. Their gang life was often organized around elaborate sexual rituals and sustained by petty crime.

Many new sources that help us contextualize and corroborate Guérin's accounts have been published in recent years. They bear witness to a dramatic increase of interest in this highly unstable period of German and European history that is due to a number of factors. The rediscovery of German avant-garde culture throughout the 1970s and 1980s has meant that Dada, the Bauhaus, expressionist theater, and biting cabaret satire have all become familiar to new generations. The appearance in Western Europe of skinheads, punks, and hardcores also recalls the politically variegated youth subculture of Germany in the early 1930s. Today, violent manifestations of racism, anti-Semitism, and homophobia have been perpetrated by those in such "uniforms," but so have antiracist and sex-positive actions, environmental awareness, and antimilitarist sentiments. The youth culture of Weimar Germany presented a similarly confusing and volatile mix, and there is an understandable desire to see if it can help us not only make sense of but fashion the present. Especially noteworthy are the many new works that reintegrate sexual politics into accounts of the Weimar Republic. Often, these are "rewritings" of earlier chronicles in which authors had deliberately suppressed the homoerotic component of their fascination with Weimar. Today, the gay movement provides a context in which many can reclaim this aspect of their youth, and there is an eagerness to integrate gay Weimar, with its militant political campaigns and thriving cultural life, into gay history.

No one, however, could have foreseen the timeliness of these new works in view of German reunification. This dramatic development, the culmination of the disintegration of the postwar legacy of spheres of influence, has provoked numerous anxieties and has kindled a desire to take a closer look at what happened the last time Germany was a single political entity. Finally, the reappearance of national and ethnic tensions that had been "pacified" by Stalinism, not only in the former Soviet Union but throughout Central and Eastern Europe, today calls for a deeper understanding of nationalist ideologies, their emancipatory as well as their exclusionist and persecutory dimensions. In all these respects, readers should find in Daniel Guérin's exciting and perspicacious account many opportunities for reflection.

When Daniel Guérin died on April 14, 1988, a memorial service was held for him at the Mur des fédérés in Paris's Père-Lachaise cemetery. This final salute at the shrine of the French Left, where fallen Communards lie side by side with the heroes of the Resistance and in the shadow of monuments to the victims of the concentration camps, was a fitting acknowledgment by Guérin's friends and comrades of his consistent presence in progressive social struggles throughout virtually the entire twentieth century. Yet, paradoxically, Guérin's stature in the French Left was as marginal as it was prestigious. This was in no small part because of his refusal to identify with either of the great parties of the French Left. Guérin maintained a highly critical relationship with the leadership of the Communist party, whose Stalinism and blind loyalty to the policies of the Soviet Union he deplored; but he also despaired of the reform-oriented politics of a Socialist leadership that recoiled before the more radical impulses of the class whose interests it claimed to represent. Likewise, Guérin took his distance from the nationalist and populist hues with which French working-class politics were often tinged; nor could he abide the vanguardism of the *groupuscules* of the far Left, many of whom he considered "frustrated" Stalinists. Sympathetic to anarchist theory, Guérin was too sophisticated a student of state power and class forces to uncritically embrace anarchist practice; yet, convinced of the revolutionary necessity of mass action, he instinctively distrusted all self-proclaimed leaderships. While he did participate in local structures of France's parties from time to time and played an active role in a "libertarian" Communist group in his later years,[1] Guérin has certainly earned the distinction of being one of the few French intellectual militants of this century to successfully negotiate the hazards of "nonaligned" status.

Guérin's independent perspective is evident in his well-known but unorthodox study of the French Revolution. Here, he broke with the traditional terms of historical debate over the relative merits of the various revolutionary leaders and celebrated instead the *bras-nus,* the bare-armed masses of Paris who demanded a deepening of the Revolution not only against Danton but even against Robespierre and Marat. For Guérin, all the celebrated leaders of the Revolution represented diverse factions of a nascent ruling class willing to tolerate popular revolt only so long as it served their interests. What they feared most, he asserted, was losing control of the masses. In most contemporary histories of the Revolution that "chose" from among these leaders, Guérin saw anachronistic, veiled apologies for Stalinism, bureaucratic control, or reformism. In turn, he was reviled by many historians for his "ultra-left" or "spontaneist" rewriting of the events in question. Yet there have been those who appreciated this radical revisionism on historical questions and its relevance to contemporary issues: When the innovative dramaturge Ariane Mnouchkine was preparing her Théâtre du Soleil's production of *1789* in celebration of the bicentennial of the Revolution, she invited Guérin to speak to her troupe, explaining that of all Guérin's books, *The Class Struggle in the First Republic* was the one he most deserved to be remembered for.[2]

---

1. In the last years of his life, Guérin belonged to the Union des travailleurs communistes libertaires (the Union of Libertarian Communist Workers), a small group on the French left that eschewed Leninist and vanguardist models of organization and action.
2. Quoted in *Libération* (Paris), April 15, 1988.

Guérin liked to say that he inherited his interest in libertarian politics from his ancestors, who included a partisan of the French revolutionary priest Babeuf and of the nineteenth-century radical Saint-Simon. Born in 1904 in Paris into a bourgeois family, Guérin was exposed from the beginning to political and cultural views that were unconventional for this milieu. His father was a friend of Marcel Proust, a Dreyfusard, and a pacifist during the First World War. He also saw to it that the young Daniel encountered other independent-minded mentors in the course of his education, both secular and religious. As a fifteen-year-old, Daniel wrote his father a detailed and critically observant postcard from the signing ceremony of the Treaty of Versailles, which formally ended the First World War and would prove to be a source of endless bitterness in Germany. As it happens, this first eyewitness *reportage* signaled a lifetime of prolific writing on politics and social history, as well as fiction, poetry, and autobiography.

Guérin became attracted to socialism during his adolescence, and at various times in his youth he belonged to the French Communist and Socialist (SFIO) parties. It was Léon Blum, a Socialist and the future prime minister of the Front populaire government, who encouraged Guérin to return to Germany in 1933 and who subsequently published a series of Guérin's articles in his newspaper, *le Populaire*. Guérin's commitment to fighting fascism also led him to write *Fascisme et grand capital* (Fascism and Big Business), the companion volume to *The Brown Plague*. Published in 1936 and then quickly translated into English, it became an important source documenting international capital's tacit or overt cooperation with Germany's National Socialists. Guérin also actively supported the French General Strike of 1936, and when his "revolutionary left" group in the Socialist party won the leadership of the Seine regional federation in 1938, he became assistant secretary.

Following the Second World War, which Guérin spent partly in Norway and then in France as part of the Trotskyist resistance, he received a grant from the French government to travel to the United States and study America's labor movement and race relations. The volumes subsequently published under the title *Où va le peuple américain?* resulted in his being banned from the United States as a "subversive" until the mid-1970s. Throughout the 1950s and 1960s Guérin played a leading role in the movement in support of anticolonial struggles. He published numerous works on this topic, appeared at countless meetings and rallies, and founded the

Committee for the Truth on Ben Barka, the kidnapped (and murdered) Moroccan opposition leader. It was also in the 1960s, dismayed by the ossification and authoritarianism of French communism, that Guérin published his own work on anarchism as well as an anthology of anarchist texts. These volumes have each been reprinted several times in many languages and are the works for which he is perhaps best known.

Unlike the leaders of the French Communist party, Guérin welcomed the student and worker uprisings that jolted France in May 1968. He was an enthusiastic participant in these events and saw in them a real hope for the rebirth of a democratic revolutionary practice. In the early 1970s, Guérin participated in the Front homosexuel d'action révolutionnaire, one of the many movements that blossomed after 1968 to take up questions traditionally shunned by the parties of the Left. In fact, Guérin's writings on homosexuality date back to the 1950s, when he published *Kinsey et la sexualité* as well as essays on literary and artistic figures. Guérin also contributed to *Arcadie,* France's early homophile journal, which began publication in 1954; with the development of a modern gay movement after 1968, he wrote regularly for the newspaper *Gai pied* and the journal *Masques.* In the 1970s Guérin published a two-volume autobiography and a "testament" in which he ascribes a central role to his homosexuality in the evolution of his political practice.

In retrospect, homoeroticism is already a powerful presence in *The Brown Plague,* both as experienced personally by Guérin and in his allusions to the way its energies are deployed in the struggle between Left and Right, above all in the battle for the loyalties of German youth. Guérin's interest in the politics and sociability of Germany in the 1930s was clearly driven by this homoerotic component, which could not be part of his stated interests when the texts were first published. After all, the original articles were destined for French daily and weekly newspapers of the Left, where homosexuality was hardly considered a serious vantage point from which to write. In fact, any hint of what was derisively called *pédérastie* (despite André Gide's courageous defense in *Corydon*), a vice associated with "decadent" figures of the aristocracy and the upper bourgeoisie, would probably have discredited Guérin's accounts altogether. Yet, it is worth recording that when I was preparing this translation, Guérin confirmed in personal conversations that the sexually charged ambiance of Germany's youth culture exerted a powerful magnetic force upon him at the time, even though he then told himself that it was a less specifically eroticized and more diffuse "militancy" that primarily attracted him.

Perhaps it is this undercurrent of homoeroticism, as well as the way the volume focuses on cultural rather than strictly political issues, that explains why *La Peste brune* has had to wait so long for its English translation. How else are we to account for the fact that unlike *Fascisme et grand capital*, which was translated almost immediately by the Trotskyist Pathfinder Press, *La Peste brune* has never been taken up by any English-language left-wing press (although it has been translated into several other languages), despite its availability in various compilations since the end of the Second World War? If *The Brown Plague* was considered insufficiently "political" in the past, that is hardly a defensible position today; it fairly resonates with contemporary concerns. The sense of urgency driving the narrative should be almost palpable to the contemporary reader, while the breadth of testimony in *The Brown Plague* bears fitting witness to the resourcefulness, tenacity, and commitment that characterized Guérin throughout his life.

The Making of a Young Radical

When Daniel Guérin set out on his walking tour in the summer of 1932, he was a neophyte neither to travel nor to Germany. Guérin's first trip abroad, in 1921, had already taken him to Mainz for an intensive German course and an exhilarating first experience away from his family. The choice of Germany, particularly so soon after the end of the First World War, would not have been an obvious one for a son of the French middle class, and Guérin undoubtedly had Marcel, his "anarcho-pacificist" father (as Daniel was later to call him), to thank for it. Balking at the chauvinist spirit of the First World War, Marcel Guérin refused to take part in patriotic demonstrations; revolted by the absurd slaughter, he obtained a first-aid certificate as early as 1914 and cared for injured soldiers, both French and German.

In his autobiography, Daniel recalls feeling guilty upon viewing the wounded soldiers brought into the luxurious Carlton Hotel in Biarritz during the First World War. His remorse at leading a "pampered life" became particularly acute when Paris was threatened in 1918 and the Guérin family went south for the second time during the war. Daniel felt shame at abandoning the city while others had to stay behind. While performing his military service in the early 1920s, he was once again embarrassed by the class privilege that allowed him to enroll as a student officer and eventually become a sublieutenant. He recalls being constantly and uncomfortably aware of the class conflicts that erupted between officers and infantrymen.

Throughout the 1920s Daniel traveled often, embarking upon itineraries befitting the education of a well-off young man of the period. He first went to Italy in 1923, and the following year to Greece. On the boat, he met his "first" Bolshevik: "I'll always remember especially how disparagingly he spoke about the French Communist leadership, and the very high opinion he held of Trotsky," Guérin says in his autobiography (1971:143). Once again, it seems this encounter with the new Soviet state was not entirely unprepared for: when the Russian tsar abdicated in February 1917, Marcel Guérin did not share his countrymen's fear for the future of the Allied war effort and instead openly celebrated the event in front of his son.

Travel also led to Daniel's "homoerotic awakening," which he remembers as occurring in the presence of the art of ancient Greece, as well as on a trip to Pompeii spent in the company of an American painter and his Florentine lover, Lelio. This Mediterranean summer left a deep impression, and when the opportunity arose in 1927 to become the director of the Beirut branch of the Agence générale de librairie, Guérin eagerly accepted. "I set out for a succession of unknown lands: the Orient, Islam, Asia, decolonization, and beyond, socialism" (1971:183). While in Beirut, Guérin preferred to live in the Arab quarter. He also developed friendships with other French colonials, including artists, teachers, archaeologists, and diplomats who were empathetic with the indigenous culture.

Guérin's political and sentimental education did not take place entirely abroad in the 1920s. In the fall of 1921 he entered the Ecole des Sciences Politiques and the Faculty of Law, where he attended the Molé-Toqueville lectures, characterized by him as a "miniature parliament." The result: a profound and lasting disillusionment with parliamentarism! The following year he wrote his thesis on the political evolution of the nineteenth-century French romantic poet Alphonse de Lamartine. Lamartine's liberal views and support for revolutionary movements made this topic quite appropriate for a young man harboring both literary and progressive political ambitions. In 1923, Guérin attended the debates in the Assemblée nationale on France's occupation of Germany's industrial heartland, the Ruhr Valley. When the Socialist leader Léon Blum rose to speak in opposition, the deputies of the Right began to chant, "Jew! Jew!" This would confirm

Guérin in his father's hostility to the anti-Semitic Right, a conviction Guérin père had held since the Dreyfus affair. In 1927, just before leaving for Beirut, Guérin had what he calls his first true political awakening when he participated in the mass demonstrations in Paris that followed the execution in Boston of the Italo-American anarchists Sacco and Vanzetti.

While Daniel's classmates went on to assume positions in French politics and the upper echelons of the civil service, he set out on a different course. His first job, as a bank clerk, disgusted him, but his second position, in a bookstore in a working-class neighborhood of Paris, was more fulfilling. Here, he began his career at the bottom of the ladder. He eventually moved into the area and participated in the political life of the local Socialist and Communist party cells. Guérin recounts how he felt "pushed toward the people" and wanted to be "surrounded by young faces, never to gaze upon death." This new orientation in his life, however, was largely propelled by the conscious recognition of his homosexual desire and the formulation of it as a politically transgressive practice. "I was throwing down the gauntlet to my class," he remembers. He began to cruise for young men in his new neighborhood and remembers falling in love with a bodybuilder and selling hand-corrected proofs of a volume by Proust just to please him! In the same year, Guérin read *Corydon,* André Gide's apologia of homosexual love, and wrote him a letter of gratitude.

Even here, however, Guérin would not be making a complete break from his family. Daniel's father eventually confessed his own homosexuality to his son, and suddenly a series of episodes from childhood made sense, including a letter Daniel discovered in which his father defends Prince Eulenberg of Germany, the focus of an orchestrated scandal in the years 1907–9 which sought to discredit an antimilitarist circle around the Kaiser. The scandal assumed major proportions as German Social Democrats fueled antiaristocratic sentiments with shameless antihomosexual attacks, in disregard of their alleged support for the decriminalization of homosexuality!

For Guérin's father, homosexuality was a "burden," but this is an attitude Daniel would firmly reject. Sexual activity among working-class boys both excited Guérin and seemed free of the sentimental and tortured travails of his own class. In his autobiography, he expresses nostalgia for Paris's *bal-musettes,* "where a male escort could licitly appear in public with another chap who felt no need whatsoever to play the queen" (1971:169).

Two boys who met at such a neighborhood event would think nothing of renting a hotel room for a few hours of sex, although the word *homosexual* would never be mentioned, its identity-giving power remaining firmly on the other side of the class line. But if boys felt relatively free to engage in sex because it didn't seem inextricably linked to a social identity, Guérin notes that a sufficient stigma existed to prevent most of them from discussing their adventures with their closest friends or cruising in their immediate neighborhoods.[3]

The Daniel Guérin who set out for Germany in 1932, then, had already had formative political and sexual experiences. Disillusioned with his native France, he left in search of a more dynamic situation. The French elections of 1932 had dislodged a regime based on the parties of the traditional Right and replaced it with one that depended upon a parliamentary alliance of radicals and Socialists. The world depression that began with the Wall Street crash had finally caught up with France, but the inability of the new regime to act any differently than its predecessor in the sphere of the economy, and its predeliction for internal maneuvering aimed at avoiding rather than assuming responsibility for the crisis, gave rise to an overwhelming antiparliamentary sentiment on all sides. A certain number of French nonconformists rose to reject the classical cleavages of French society played out during the 1920s, leading to much talk of "reconstruction" after the period of postwar "degeneration." Eventually, most (though by no means all) of these intellectuals would drift to the right with the polarizations of the late 1930s, and many would support the collaborationist regime at Vichy during the Second World War.

The French writer Robert Brasillach's memoir of the interwar years, *Notre avant-guerre,* provides a lucid and vivid account of this drift. Guérin and Brasillach were essentially of the same generation, but their itineraries could not have diverged more dramatically. Brasillach's experiences of Parisian schools and the capital's political intrigue led him to a generationally typical rejection of parliamentarism, which he equates with "la folie démocratique." For Brasillach, though, an ill-defined populism eventually gives way to a strong bond with the reactionary Charles Maurras and his Action

3. These recollections were made by Guérin during a conversation I had with him at his summer home in La Ciotat in July 1984, but a similar account is available in *Son Testament* (102–4).

française movement. Even though Brasillach regrets the disappearance of interwar Parisian culture—"vivante, brillante, gracieuse et folle" (98)—his account is riddled with racist and anti-Semitic complaints about the "decadence" eating away at France's national resolve: "Paul Morand showed us [in his writings] the head of the American Negro poised over our moribund society (122); "Behind Le Corbusier lurked the profile of Monsieur Lévitan" (15). The specters of "international communism," "international Jewry," and German rearmament led Brasillach to the conclusion that France must nurture its own, specifically *French* form of national socialism. After the liberation of France, Brasillach would be tried and executed as a collaborator.

On the other hand, a renewed interest in spirituality also produced commitments to social justice and individual responsibility through "personalist" theology of the kind exemplified by Emmanuel Mounier and his journal, *Esprit.* Guérin rejected this orientation as well, satisfied that he had resolved his own spiritual "crises" while he was a student. Instead, he looked to the heroic class conflicts that seemed to be shaping up across the Rhine. A return to the land of his first travels held out the promise of an intoxicating mix of political and erotic involvements and the opportunity to be "useful" by reporting on the fascist danger to his complacent and lethargic compatriots.

The Lure of Germany

Guérin's autobiographical accounts of his travels in Weimar Germany are contemporaneous with an impressive body of similar Anglo-American works, supplemented in recent years by translations from the German as well as by new memoirs. Many of these are more preoccupied by literary and aesthetic concerns than *The Brown Plague,* and some have enjoyed great success through popularization in film and musical dramas. Christopher Isherwood's *Goodbye to Berlin,* for example, has served as the basis for two films—*I Am a Camera* and *Cabaret,* originally a Broadway musical; and the popular film *Julia* was based on Lillian Hellman's suspenseful account of the early Nazi years. Despite their adamant hostility to Nazism, these productions all contribute to the disparaging view of the Weimar Republic as "decadent," a kind of rotten apple waiting to fall into Hitler's hands. Similarly, the American writer Glenway Wescott returned from Europe in the early 1930s with "fear and trembling," the title he gave to his subsequent account of the voyage. His lurid account of a generalized European madness (as set off against "America") is conveyed with detachment yet alarm: "An ancient civilization talking nonsense and getting drunk, painting its face with furious young colours, raving like an adolescent lover, threatening to commit murder right and left, finally rolling all by itself on the floor, in a panic and a fit of morbid anger, its feet hammering its stomach in, one of its wild arms killing the other, until it is at least half dead—in that light, in the mirror of the mind, the sight of the beloved civilization in which . . . we are included, is enough to drive us all mad" (Wescott, 323).

While many writers, including Wescott, Isherwood, and Stephen Spender, convey their experience of Weimar in terms of an increasing "self-knowledge" revealed through confronting the horrors of the impending conflagration, Guérin's account is consonant with a wealth of recent material that provides a more complex, nuanced view of a period in German politics that knew both successes and failures. Because the unique features of *The Brown Plague* are better appreciated through a comparison with the "Berlin stories" of his contemporaries, it is worth taking some time to examine the fascination that Weimar in its decline exercised on young foreigners with political, cultural, and erotic preoccupations.

In many ways, young nonconformist writers coming to Weimar Germany were all impressed by the same things. The key word seemed to be *modern*. In his autobiographical account *World Within World* (1951), the British poet Stephen Spender qualifies German modernism as a "popular mass movement" among the generation that came of age after the defeat of the First World War. This defeat had resulted in the downfall of the Reich and the proclamation of the Republic, which itself had to contend with strangling inflation in the early 1920s. "Perhaps they thought that their generation had been purged of the bourgeois ideal of accumulated property by the great inflation of 1923," Spender muses. "Now their aims were to live simply from day to day, and to enjoy to the utmost everything that was free: sun, water, friendship, and their bodies" (107).

Spender's time in Germany was spent largely in the thriving, no-holds-barred port city of Hamburg, where he first arrived in 1929. "There were buildings, with broad clean vertical lines crossed by strong horizontals, which drove into the sky like railroads" (108). Indeed, Guérin's awe before the audacious architecture of the trade union buildings is at once echoed and amplified in Spender's account. Modernism in Germany was "stripped down" in more than an architectural sense, however. More than the sum of its parts, it was an unabashed "life of the senses, a sunlit garden from which sin was excluded" (107).

In Hamburg, Spender quickly gained the friendship of the young photographer Herbert List (fictionalized in the novel *The Temple* as Joachim Lenz) and was introduced to his circle of friends at parties in List's sparsely but impeccably furnished modern apartment. The guests "were bronze-skinned and they dressed with a simplicity which suggested leaves and summer. The boys seemed girlish whilst the girls seemed masculine" (110). In a more recent essay, Spender adds that List's apartment "suggested naked flesh and easy physical relations between youths who seemed to have stepped out of the Parthenon frieze" (*Herbert List: Junge Männer*, 1988: Introd., 1).

Spender eventually went to Berlin and joined the novelist Christopher Isherwood, who had already traveled there to be with Wystan (W. H.) Auden. Unlike Spender, Isherwood lived poorly in one of the city's most derelict districts. In his fictionalized memoir, *Christopher and His Kind* (1976), Isherwood remembers that "Berlin meant boys." This account offers vivid evocations of the many gay bars in Berlin's working-class districts, far from "officially decadent Berlin" in the tourist-infested West End. Christopher came here because he "was suffering from an inhibition, then not unusual among upper-class homosexuals; he couldn't relax sexually with a member of his own class or nation. He needed a working-class foreigner" (10). What Isherwood found were young working-class boys who prostituted themselves and at the same time hungered for "a Friend— that sacred German concept." "This friend would help them with money, of course, but he would also—and this was far more important to them— offer them serious interest, advice, encouragement [but] from the average client's point of view, these boys had no future; therefore one couldn't allow oneself to care what became of them" (32).

Like Isherwood, Guérin was sexually drawn to young working-class men, and his writing is similarly suffused with an infatuation for "the

German Boy" or "the Wanderer" that harkens back to an older cult of nature.[4] In the narrative, one senses Guérin's attraction to these youths and to what Spender would call some fifty years later their "pervasive sexuality, a kind of aura that shone from their bodies . . . something one felt about them whether they were dressed or undressed" (1980:8).

As a politically conscious young man, Guérin was also aware of Germany's gay movement, the world's most advanced. Jim Steakley's important work, *The Homosexual Emancipation Movement in Germany,* provides a detailed account of the Weimar years, during which some thirty periodicals for homosexuals regularly appeared. Dr. Magnus Hirschfeld's Institute of Sexual Science in Berlin was internationally renowned. Here, Hirschfeld propagated his "third sex" theory and advocated the decriminalization of homosexuality in Germany. As a homosexual, a Jew, and a Social Democrat, Hirschfeld became an obvious target for vilification by the Nazis. His institute was raided in May 1933, and books, files, and a bust of him were publicly burned a few days later, an event Isherwood witnessed. Over the years, this spectacle has been seen by millions in newsreel accounts, yet, until recently, mention has seldom been made of the precise nature of the materials destroyed.

Another leader in the fight against paragraph 175 of the German penal code, which outlawed homosexual activities, was Kurt Hiller, who, in a paraphrase of Marx, insisted that "the liberation of homosexuals can only be the work of homosexuals themselves." The Communist deputies cast the deciding votes when a parliamentary committee finally voted to delete this paragraph in 1929, but the New York stock market crash disrupted the agenda of the Reichstag and the bill was never brought to a full vote. In the closing years of Weimar, the campaign never regained its momentum, and as Isherwood notes, "a contradiction between personal and collective liberation emerged, for it was far easier to luxuriate in the concrete utopia of the

4. Howard Becker's *German Youth: Bond or Free* (1946) is a fascinating historical and mythical account, albeit stylistically idiosyncratic and highly homophobic, that seeks to demonstrate that certain elements of this tradition may be drawn on for the purposes of social reconstruction. Also see Hermann Giesecke's *Vom Wandervogel bis zur Hitlerjugend* (Munich: Juventa Verlag, 1981) and the photo study edited by Winfried Mogge, *Bilder aus dem Wandervogel Leben: Jugendbewegung in Fotos von Julius Gross* (Cologne: Verlag Wissenschaft und Politik, 1986).

urban subculture than to struggle for an emancipation which was apparently only formal and legalistic" (1976:81). Despite the fact that certain leading Nazi figures, including sa leader Ernst Röhm,[5] were known to be homosexual, the party's shrill response on being canvassed on its views toward homosexuality ought to have served as sufficient warning of the persecutions to come should the Nazis ever assume power: "Anyone who even thinks of homosexual love is our enemy," they warned. "We reject anything that emasculates our people and makes it a plaything for our enemies, for we know that life is a fight and it's madness to think that men will ever embrace fraternally. . . . [H]omosexuality . . . robs us of our last chance to free our people from the bondage which now enslaves it" (in Steakley, 84). The particular naïveté with which such vituperations were dismissed or ignored was fatal to Weimar, a society in which Spender had vainly searched for a "political will to survive" among the cultural splendors and advanced attitudes.

For Spender, 1929 was the last year of that "strange Indian summer" before "everything became politics" (*The Temple,* 1988: Introd., x–xi). Whether German youth remained in the cities as the crisis deepened or set out as *Wandervögel* (Birds of Passage), hiking along Germany's roads, the privations of the period eventually caught up with them. In the early 1930s, "what became of youth" was increasingly sinister. Many of the wanderers Spender had met on the banks of the Rhine were being enlisted in Hitler Youth groups and Storm Trooper sections.[6] He never forgot the eeriness of sunbathing on the shores of one of Berlin's many lakes with other "children of the sun" while listening to the sounds of Nazi military exercises in the forest beyond.

As the violent behavior of the Storm Trooper sections became better

---

5. Hitler had Röhm, a popular and charismatic figure, murdered on the Night of the Long Knives (June 30, 1934). His death signaled the beginning of a significant escalation in the persecution of homosexuals by the Nazis, although from the beginning of the Third Reich, gay establishments came under attack and "vice" charges rose steeply. Gay concentration camp inmates were assigned the pink triangle badge, which has since become the emblem of the modern gay liberation movement.

6. In *The Temple,* Joachim's lover Heinrich, who had originally left his Bavarian village to avoid being a financial burden on his parents, gives up wandering, his boyfriend, and hedonism; he finds work as a clerk in a store and becomes a Nazi.

known and Nazi race ideology more triumphalist, several observers began to explore possible links among these contemporary cultural manifestations and archaic aspects of Germanic societies. The Italian historian Carlo Ginzburg examines this literature and asks us to think more carefully about the extent to which "the assumption of an ideological continuity between Indo-European mythology in its Germanic variant and the political, institutional, and social realities of the Third Reich contribute to a better understanding of the latter" (1990:134). In the 1930s, many in France were tempted to see in the youthful Storm Troopers and the adult Nazi leadership the most recent avatars of ancient *Männerbünde* (male societies). In this paradigm, the young Nazis are likened to the *berserkir*—"the 'young' [who] assume in the life of Germanic societies [the] function of tumult and of violence" (129) while the adults, like the Germanic chiefs in this ideal of social equilibrium, represent "the equalizing, conservative element working for order" (130). Ginzburg demonstrates how self-serving such claims were for Nazi theorists—how they had taken the "empty vessel" of Indo-European ideology and filled it with their own poisonous brew.[7] Nevertheless, many outside Germany, particularly in France, were only too willing to praise the Nazis' "discipline" of the nation's youth and bemoaned the fact that their own countries lacked structures akin to the Hitler Youth or the SA that could be justified with recourse to archaic national mythologies and "personalities."[8]

Although Guérin in no way shared these regrets, he was unable to deny the kindling of desire that the accoutrements and ritual of Nazi youth culture stirred in him. Thus, while Christopher Isherwood would eventually take himself to task for squandering the opportunity to develop an appropriate "psychological interest" in the Nazi High Command (1976:94), Guérin sought out occasions to see the Nazi leadership interact with its

7. A primary concern of Ginzburg in this essay is to extricate Georges Dumézil's *Mythes et Dieux des Germains* from this body of literature and rescue it from the more general co-optation of *histoire de longue durée* by partisans of the New Right. He demonstrates that there is a world of difference between identifying archaic, mythological paradigms and acquiescing to the particular uses to which they are put in various ideological projects.

8. See, for example, the pamphlet by General Weygand, *Comment élever nos fils?*, in which the future Vichyiste expresses admiration not only for the Hitler Youth but also for youth groups in fascist Italy and (somewhat more grudgingly) Soviet Russia.

public. His particular attention to Nazi spectacle seems motivated precisely by a "psychological interest" in the ambivalent and contradictory feelings of sexual attraction and political revulsion he felt before the armies of their sculpted, leather-clad, youthful disciples.

Guérin had no illusions, however, about the authoritarian and brutalizing command the Nazis were set to impose on German youth, and he especially mourned the violence being done to the gentle, comradely side of the German youth culture. And, of course, the only discipline to which Daniel Guérin was politically reconciled was to be found in the fighting spirit of young proletarians affiliated with the Communist and Social Democratic parties, a form of activism for which he knew many young wanderers were unsuited. Guérin clearly regretted the extent to which all aspects of the youth culture had been distorted by political polarization, yet he would never have countenanced Stephen Spender's young friend's refusal to vote for the Communists in 1932 out of disapproval for their tendency to judge everything as being "for or against politics."[9] For Guérin, everything *had* become politics, and the question now was whether there were time and means to save Germany from the Brown tide preparing to swamp it.

Germany in 1932

Guérin arrived in Germany in the closing year of what Spender calls the Weimardämmerung (1951:129), the twilight of the Republic. Field Marshal Paul von Hindenburg had already been elected the Republic's second president in 1925, a signal that the "old Germany" was far from defeated by the new. In fact, Germany's traditional elites, including landowners, noblemen, and the High Command, were deliberately steering the Weimar Republic toward a system with increased presidential power. With no commitment to parliamentary democracy and a preference for authoritarian rule, these elements took every opportunity to weaken the legislative

---

9. In *The Temple,* Joachim (Herbert List) says, "[T]he Communists could not tolerate a person like me who lives for things that have nothing to do with politics. They regard everything and everyone as political, in being either for them or against them. I don't want to live in a world where whatever I do is judged as being either for or against politics. Even if I agreed with the Communists about everything else, I couldn't agree about that" (151).

effectiveness of the Reichstag, where, not coincidentally, the Left also had its greatest political influence (see Noakes and Pridham, 88–89).[10]

Weimar's last majority government collapsed in the wake of the 1929 "Krasch" and was replaced until 1932 by the regime of Chancellor Heinrich Brüning. Rule by presidential emergency decree became more the rule than the exception, leading Stephen Spender to truculently characterize Brüning's government as "a kind of rallying place of frightened people" (1951:129). Hindenburg dismissed Brüning in May 1932 and replaced him with Franz von Papen, who was in turn briefly succeeded by Kurt von Schleicher in December 1932. In rapid order, these governments, based on various factions of the country's conservative elites, attempted to impose their reactionary solutions on a society racked by massive inflation and unemployment.[11] A series of laws sought to drastically reduce social benefits and generally constrain the welfare state developed by Weimar Social Democratic governments to cope with the first inflationary period in the early 1920s. Restrictions were imposed on trade union rights and other democratic freedoms, including measures justified in the name of job stimulation that allowed employers who hired the unemployed to pay them wages lower than those stipulated in union contracts (Heiden, 487). With no majority coalition possible, the Reichstag remained stalemated when confronted with these measures. In the meantime, the Nazis actually lost votes in the November 1932 elections. Throughout that year they struggled with severe financial difficulties and the increasing dissatisfaction of a base that continually saw itself denied the state power that seemed to be within its grasp. To make matters worse, Nazi candidates were often met with organized hostility on their campaign tours, as a plaintive excerpt from Joseph Goebbels's diary relates: "Now we travel in disguise. . . . We have to

10. The result, according to the historian Karl Dietrich Bracher, was that "the government was weakened by the more and more drastic exclusions of the parliamentary, democratic organs and by the narrowly bureaucratic character of the presidential system, which went its own way . . . ignoring public opinion and the political mood of the governed masses" (Bracher, 112).

11. In fact, Germany "bottomed out" in 1931 when real wages were at their lowest level and unemployment was at its highest since the war. By late 1932, orders from abroad had begun to increase and German war reparations were finally canceled. Konrad Heiden aptly points to the irony of the situation: "The victors of Versailles had given the Reichswehr [i.e., Chancellor General Schleicher] what they had denied the democratic ministers of the German Republic!" (509).

take a side-street to keep from falling into the hands of the Communists who have occupied all the other entrances. . . . In Elberfeld the Red press has called the mob into the streets. The approaches to the stadium are blocked off completely. . . . I must leave my own native city like a criminal, pursued by curses, abuse, vilification, stoned, and spat upon" (in Heiden, 469–70).

In these last free elections, the two major parties of the Left, the Social Democrats and the Communists, received a total of 37.8 percent of the vote, with the Communists making new gains. The Center party, supported by the Catholic workers' movement, received 12 percent. In the final year of Weimar, workers remained largely opposed to the Nazis, who managed to obtain only 33.6 percent of the vote, a significant portion of which came from middle-class former supporters of the traditional conservative parties. Unlike many others, Guérin was not lulled into a false sense of optimism by these results, however tempting this may have been. After all, when he had set out for Germany a few months earlier, he was fully prepared to be swept off his feet by Europe's mightiest, most cultured proletariat. It is clear that he sympathized with the view held by many Marxists in his time that the Revolution "ought" to have happened first in Germany, and Guérin might well have felt that the menace of Nazism would finally provide the setting for a "battle of the gods" worthy of a heroic emancipatory class. Instead, he discovered much idealism and energy at the base, but a complacent trade union and Social Democratic party (SPD) leadership. The SPD leaders were, on the average, considerably older than their general membership and were steeped in parliamentarism to the exclusion of other forms of political mobilization.[12] Ominously, they were uncomfortable with the formation of the Reichsbanner and Iron Front self-defense brigades aimed at countering the increasing violence of antirepublican forces and Nazi Storm Troopers. Their refusal to mobilize these brigades on July 20, when Reich Chancellor von Papen declared a state of emergency in Prussia and deposed the state's SPD government, proved costly indeed. A final opportunity to extend the resistance against foes of the Republic had been squandered at the very moment when, in Erich

---

12. Following the collapse of the Müller government in 1930, the SPD Reichstag deputy Julius Leber wrote, "For the first time an intense dissatisfaction with [their] leadership was discernible in the ranks of the Social Democrats" (in Matthias, 54).

Matthias's apt assessment, "a total failure could not have been more disastrous than the political and psychological effects of inactivity" (Matthias, 62).

As for the Communist party (KPD), it attracted militants from the most destitute sectors of the working class, but they were guided by leaders often more intent on fighting the SPD "social fascists" than the Nazis. The Communist leadership came to view Nazism as a necessary transitional stage on the road to proletarian dictatorship. A decisive, shocking experience with fascism would galvanize the working class, causing it to regroup and overthrow this most extreme excrescence of the capitalist crisis. In this scenario, the SPD's continuing hold on large segments of the working class became the primary obstacle to the proper unfolding of history. Accordingly, KPD Reichstag leader Ernst Torgler rebuffed last-minute SPD entreaties to form a united front against the Nazis: "It doesn't even enter our heads. The Nazis must take power. Then in four weeks the whole working class will be united under the leadership of the Communist Party" (in Heiden, 551–52).[13] Finally, as the German-born American historian Fritz Stern has noted, many on the left—and not just Communists—believed that if Hitler were to come to power, the repression that would follow would be bearable. In their optimism they even wagered that "a period of martyrdom [might] perhaps bring about a heroic renewal. [T]he Left did not anticipate the terror with which the National Socialists, if ever in power, would destroy all opposition, real or imagined" (Stern, 126).

In the final analysis, the collapse of Weimar cannot be accounted for through either a narrowly economistic reading of the conditions prevailing in the early 1930s or an exclusive focus on the sorry factionalism of the Left. The German sociologist Detlev Peukert notes that the closing years of the Weimar period were marked by a general social decline variously interpreted as the breakup of capitalism, the disintegration of traditional values, or the "Decline of the West." While people may have disagreed about the causes and solutions of this decline, everyone seemed to agree that "on the

---

13. The views of the Soviet government and the Communist International consistently echoed this conviction. Even after the Nazi victory, the Comintern seemed more encouraged than shaken by the extraordinary levels of brutality and repression wielded by the new regime. On April 1, 1933, it adopted a resolution claiming that "the open Fascist dictatorship[. . .] had freed the masses from the influence of Social Democracy and thus accelerated the tempo of evolution of Germany toward proletariat revolution" (Heiden, 552).

level of everyday life [matters] could not continue as they had done hitherto" (Peukert, 27). The simultaneity of the collapse of the Weimar political system, the massive economic convulsion, and the upheaval of traditional social values placed unprecedented strain on German society. While Weimar had successfully integrated the "labor aristocracy" into political life through the trade unions and the Social Democratic party, the same period also saw the middle classes lose their privileged role. According to Peukert, the humiliations of inflation impelled them to increasingly detach themselves from the established political culture. Other "free-floating elements" included the young, the long-term unemployed (especially veterans), and even an entirely new but disoriented modern "white-collar" middle class composed of employees in commerce, social and public service, and technological jobs. How could these layers make sense of a project of modernization gone awry? Peukert summarizes: "It was the whole 'system' that was evil, purely and simply. . . . The causes, since in reality they were obscure and genuinely hard to separate out, were personalised and mythologised. There had to be a 'conspiracy' " (41).

Such sentiments were the very lifeblood of the Nazis, who did not hesitate to name the "conspirators": Jews, Marxists, and the so-called November criminals.[14] They pointed to a single document as evidence of this collective plot: the Treaty of Versailles. Signed in 1919 at the conclusion of the First World War, the treaty imposed large reparations on Germany, dictated its demilitarization, and reapportioned substantial territories of the former Reich to other powers. Chauvinist politicians in the victor nations boasted unceasingly about Germany's defeat, and the French occupation of the Ruhr Valley in 1923 delivered a devastating setback just as Germany was emerging from a period of staggering postwar inflation. Many intellectuals and militants across Europe, from liberals to Communists, knew that the treaty terms were exacerbating social tensions and national resentments in Germany. In Spender's novel *The Temple,* the autobiographical character Paul is revolted by the Nazis' ability to exploit this situation: "It was terrible to see real grievances being exploited to justify evil ends," he says (*The Temple,* 1988:162).

---

14. So called for the armistice with the Allied forces on November 11, 1918. German militarists and ultranationalists contended that Germany had not actually lost the war; it had been betrayed and "sold out" by those who capitulated and sued for peace.

Hitler promised to "redeem" Germany and crush those who attacked it from within and without. He promised a "fundamental break with the system" and an "awakening," the very terms used by many of those who profess their faith in Hitler to Guérin. Whether recalling their elation at having caught a glimpse of a Nazi leader at a mass rally or expressing humiliation and feelings of persecution at the hands of France and the other Allied victors, many of the townspeople encountered by Guérin on his first trip confirm Peukert's contention that Nazism's charisma "was the combined outcome of the experience of crisis, the yearning for security and the desire for aggression, all merged into a breathless dynamism that latched onto whatever was the most immediate event. . . . The more distant future could look after itself" (42).

In retrospect, it may seem difficult to comprehend how the pillars of the "old" Germany could be so cynical and arrogant about their ability to manipulate Hitler and his brown-shirted masses. Certainly the Nazis' disarray in 1932 made the party less fearful to the conservative elites, who now entertained the possibility of enlisting it as a "disciplinary force" against the working class while pursuing their own reactionary agendas. Likewise, the Nazis' lack of a coherent program fostered the illusion that they could be made subservient to other counterrevolutionary projects.[15] And as Fritz Stern suggests, the traditional Left was also in thrall to a fatal misrecognition, adjusting Hitler "to their own limited imagination" and seeing in him merely "a caricature of something old and known" (125).

Strikingly, *The Brown Plague* does not partake in this general tendency; nor does Guérin ever adopt the convenient but misleading characterization of the Communists and Nazis as two "extremes" doing violence against the Republic. Above all, he is astounded by the strategic bankruptcy of the Left, especially its historic failure to unite in the face of the Nazis' determination—already confirmed through countless "previews"—to crush the parties and organizations of the working class by using terror and murder as linchpins of their future regime. Years later, Guérin would recall in his autobiography how "the crushing defeat—which was also ours [in

---

15. Guérin's descriptions of the Territorial soldiers, the *Herren* (gentlemen), and the caucuses of the conservative parties in the Reichstag bring to mind the vicious sketches by George Groz, especially in his *Das Gesicht der Herrschenden Klasse* (Berlin: Malik-Verlag, 1921).

France]—filled me with a despair born not of discouragement or passivity but of rage" (1977:25).

1933: Germany under the Nazis

In the short period between Daniel Guérin's departure from Germany in 1932 and his return in 1933, the balance between two worlds tilted definitively in favor of Nazi barbarism. Hitler had been chancellor for just three months when Daniel Guérin returned to Germany at the end of April 1933. He arrived just as two spectacular events were taking place that would mark the demise of the organized cultural life of the working class as it had developed there since the mid-nineteenth century. First, on May 1, the day after Guérin's arrival, Germany celebrated its newly proclaimed National Day of Labor. Contrary to the Social Democratic governments of the Weimar Republic that had never seen fit to legally sanction May Day as the international workers' holiday—and perhaps shied away from doing so because of the day's Communist associations—the Nazis boldly and cynically appropriated May Day for their own propagandistic ends. Then, on May 2, the offices of the trade unions were occupied and their structures absorbed into the new state-sponsored German Labor Front.

Guérin's account is particularly effective in communicating the loss these events symbolized to workers the world over, and to his French compatriots in particular. In Germany, working-class political loyalties entailed far more than casting a vote from time to time. Adherence to either the Social Democratic party, which traced its origins to the great founders of socialism, or to the Communist party, founded by Rosa Luxemburg and Karl Liebknecht after the Social Democrats voted in favor of arms credits for the pursuit of the First World War, made one part of a cultural community, not just a narrowly political one. Each party boasted a range of services and institutions that embraced its millions of members from the cradle to the grave: community health projects; relief and charitable works; educational programs; musical, theatrical, cinematic, and literary activities; sports clubs; vacation colonies; travel exchange programs; libraries; clubs for children of different age groups; women's organizations; a network of local, regional, and national newspapers and magazines; housing cooperatives; and self-defense militias.

This world was now snuffed out by what Christopher Isherwood (who like Guérin also returned to Germany at the end of April) describes as the "terror in the air." The new political climate was a far cry from the "blessing in disguise" many of Isherwood's acquaintances had hoped for when President Hindenburg finally named Hitler chancellor on January 30. Isherwood expresses astonishment at their naïve conviction that Hitler would be exposed relatively quickly and the Nazis promptly discredited. In reality, the National Socialists had long prepared for this *Machtergreifung* (assumption of power) by establishing military and political command structures parallel to those of the state; one set of institutions would be grafted onto the other in a matter of months.[16] Even though Hitler at first headed a coalition government with only two other Nazi ministers (out of a total of twelve)[17] and nominally served a president who would not even speak to him unless the aristocratic Vice Chancellor von Papen was also present, the real relationship of political forces was far more favorable to Hitler. K. D. Bracher explains in his study of the process whereby Nazi structures were fused with those of the state that "the National Socialists held the Chancellery, the Reich Ministry of the Interior, the Prussian Ministry of the Interior, and—through the complaisant [Blomberg], the Reichswehr Ministry. This meant control over all the key positions needed for total "integration" (Bracher, "Stages" 115–16).

Nazification of the state was greatly facilitated by the already lengthy experience of rule by presidential decree. The Decree to Protect the German *Volk,* of February 4, for example, greatly extended police powers but was itself an expansion of the Police Administration Law of July 1931. The burning of the Reichstag on the night of February 27–28 provided the pretext for a new decree that declared a permanent state of emergency and suppressed all civil liberties. Nazi leaders were convinced that the arson actually marked the beginning of the Communist uprising they had expected for so long. According to eyewitness accounts, "After Hitler had

16. This is not to suggest that the Nazis were implementing a fully worked out plan when they assumed power. In fact, their program lacked precision on almost all the major issues, and many of the policies, laws, and decrees emitted in the opening months of the regime were improvised responses whose character was entirely ad hoc. Similarly, the Reichswehr (army) was not a stable ally of the regime until Hitler eliminated the "plebian" SA as a parallel source of violence by having Röhm and other SA leaders murdered on June 30, 1934.

17. A fourth Nazi, Joseph Goebbels, joined the cabinet as minister of propaganda on March 13, 1933, and was named deputy Führer on April 21.

recovered from a kind of cataleptic trance, he had . . . flown into an inter-minable outburst of rage and vilified the Communist 'subhumans.' . . . He declared that the Reich government would take the measures necessary to crush and exterminate this dire threat not only to Germany but to Europe as well" (in Holborn, 167–68).[18] Among the provisions of the Decree of the Reich President for the Protection of People and State that Hitler con-vinced Hindenburg to sign were restrictions on "personal liberty, on the right of free expression and opinion, including freedom of the press, on the right of assembly and association, and violations of the privacy of postal, telegraphic, and telephonic communications," while "warrants for house-searches, orders for confiscations as well as restrictions on property rights [are] permissible beyond the legal limits otherwise prescribed" (in Noakes and Pridham, 1974:174). The decree also gave the Reich government the authority to take over the functions of any state government unwilling or unable to implement measures necessary for public security.

On the night of the fire, some four thousand Communist militants were arrested, including all the party's candidates in the upcoming March 5 Reichstag elections. At the subsequent trial, and with the whole world watching, the court had to acquit all the Communist leaders accused of the "conspiracy" for lack of a shred of credible evidence. Marinus van der Lubbe, a Dutch radical who confessed to the act, was the only defendant convicted. He was executed for arson, which was proclaimed a capital offense *retroactively* to the time the fire was set! This violation of the principle of *nulla poene sine lege*[19] was completely typical of the Nazis' hostility to "legalism." As Noakes and Pridham explain, "The nature of the law as a set of rules regulating human activities with the aim of introducing rationality and predictability into social relationships was totally incom-patible with the *Führerprinzip* which formed the basis of the Nazi concept of authority. For, since the Führer regarded himself and was regarded by his movement as a man of destiny, chosen to lead Germany and expressing the will of the nation, any body of laws was viewed with suspicion as a restric-

---

18. See also the account of Rudolf Diels, the head of the Prussian political police, in Noakes and Pridham, doc. 94 (139–41).

19. "[T]he principle that no one should be tried for an act which was not an offence at the time he committed it or be given a punishment which was not stipulated for that offence at the time he committed it" (Noakes and Pridham, 481).

tion on his freedom of action" (471). The judicial apparatus was also bent to Hitler's will through the "reeducation" of judges and attorneys in Nazi ideology, and especially through the establishment of "people's courts" that did not rely on traditional rules of evidence or standards of guilt and innocence.[20]

On March 23 the logic of the *Führerprinzip* was extended to parliament itself with the adoption of the Enabling Law. Only the Socialists voted against this measure, which suspended the constitution and allowed Hitler to rule independently of parliament for four years (the Enabling Law was renewed in 1937, then again in 1939, and extended "indefinitely" in 1943).[21] On April 22, 1933, barely a month after its initial promulgation, Propaganda Minister and Deputy Führer Joseph Goebbels recorded in his diary: "The Führer's authority is now completely ascendant in the Cabinet. There will be no more voting. The Führer's personality decides. All this has been achieved much more quickly than we dared to hope" (in Noakes and Pridham, doc. 110, 163).

As for law enforcement, Minister Hermann Göring lost no time in purging the regular police of most of its nonparty leadership. He then instructed his forces that they "must in all circumstances avoid giving even the appearance of a hostile attitude, still less the impression of persecuting the patriotic associations," by which he meant the Nazi Storm Troopers, the ss,[22] and other right-wing militias. On the contrary, the "patriotic"

20. For further documentation on Nazism and the law, see Noakes and Pridham (1983: 471–89). For a contemporaneous presentation by the Nazis of their views on law and order to the outside world, see "The Administration of Justice in National Socialist Germany," by Dr. Franz Gürtner, Reich minister of justice, in *Germany Speaks,* a compendium of essays "by twenty-one Leading Members of Party and State" published in English by the Reich minister for foreign affairs (London: Thornton Butterworth, 1938).

21. The eighty-one KPD deputies would certainly have voted against the Ermächtigungsgesetz, but they were already under arrest. Twenty-six of the 120 SPD deputies could not reach the Reichstag, and the others voted surrounded by SA forces who heckled and threatened them with physical harm. After Hindenburg's death in 1934, Hitler did not assume the presidency; instead, he held a referendum to legitimate the fusing in his person of the positions of Führer of the German *Volk* and chancellor of the Reich.

22. Unlike the "plebian" SA, the SS was regarded as an elite corps from its very inception as the personal bodyguard of Hitler. As the SS expanded and garnered police powers and authority over the concentration camps, regulations proliferated aimed at guaranteeing its racial superiority (marriages were to be eugenically arranged to promote "superior" breeding).

activities of these groups were "to be supported by every means." As for the activities of "subversives," especially the Communists, these were "to be combatted with the most drastic methods. . . . [W]eapons must be used ruthlessly when necessary [and] police officers who in the execution of this duty use their firearms will be supported by [me] without regard to the effect of their shots. . . . Every official must constantly bear in mind that failure to act is more serious than errors committed in acting" (in Noakes and Pridham, 1983:136).

With Hitler in the Chancellery, the sa and the ss proceeded to engage in unbridled acts of hooliganism and terror. "Manufacturers and shopkeepers . . . [put cars] at their disposal in order to assure themselves protection. The cars of Jews and democrats were simply confiscated" (Krausnick et al., 408). Opposition political offices were destroyed and the contents of many homes broken up. An account of one such campaign in Brunswick on March 3 was published by the Social Democratic party in exile:

> The regular police had . . . blocked off the surrounding streets with a strong force. The Nazis looted the [Volksfreund] building in front of their very eyes. They destroyed the furniture and equipment. Anything that was moveable they dragged out into the yard. Documents, pieces of furniture, valuable administrative material, the book supplies of the *Volksfreund* bookshop, many hundredweight of expensive propaganda film, record, account books, and flags were heaped up on a pyre and set alight. . . . During the course of the action, the private tenants of the *Volksfreund* building were raided in their flats, abused, threatened with weapons and beaten up. . . . In the evening . . . [h]undreds of heavily armed Nazi patrols marched through the town, chased passers-by and beat up members of the public. (Noakes and Pridham, 1983: doc. 99, 148–50)

These accounts are consonant with many in the meticulously documented *Brown Book of Hitler Terror.* Published in several languages in 1933 by the World Committee for the Victims of German Fascism, the *Brown Book* was the major compendium of the horrors of the first months of the Nazi regime available to readers outside Germany at the time. In his brief introduction to this digest of persecutions, humiliations, torture, and murder, Lord Marley notes, "We would have been able to publish even worse individual cases, but we have not done this, just because they were individual cases. Not a single one of the cases published in this book is an exceptional case. Each case cited is typical" (9).

Attached to the state as auxiliary police, the Nazi forces were able to cordon off entire working-class neighborhoods, remove militants and systematically beat them, then return them to their homes under threats of death should they reveal what had happened to them. In the early weeks of the regime, victims of the SA and the SS were spirited off to makeshift, or "wild," camps, often located in abandoned factory buildings and warehouses. The total number of such "revenge arrests" remains unknown, but the anxiety provoked by these "disappearances" and the suffering, silence, and destitution (since they were sure to lose their jobs) of those who were released served the intended deterrent function.[23] It did not take long for these improvised torture centers to be replaced by officially sanctioned camps for the *Schutzhaft* (protective detention) of "elements hostile to the state." The opening of Dachau concentration camp outside Munich was announced on March 30 and duly reported by the press in Germany and throughout Europe. The introduction to Dachau's "Regulations for Discipline and Punishment" stipulates that "tolerance means weakness. In light of this conception, punishment will be mercilessly handed out whenever the interests of the Fatherland warrant it." In fact, punishment, which included public floggings, hangings, and long periods of solitary confinement in minuscule concrete cells, was a regular and predictable part of camp life guaranteed through a series of contradictory rules of behavior and deliberate provocations by guards. Dachau's internal regime would become the prototype for all future camps, including Oranienburg, the installation outside Berlin visited by Guérin.[24]

In the early months of the regime, the vast majority of camp internees were political opponents, mainly Communists and Social Democrats. In

23. "Deterrence" resulted in a flood of resignations from the workers' parties. "I see no other solution but my resignation," wrote Hans J. to the SPD in Hanover. "The existence of my family is at stake. If the fate of unemployment, which in my experience can be *very, very* hard, is unavoidable, I need not reproach myself for not having done everything in the interests of my wife and child." Another worker resigned with the promise to "try to live for my job, my family and my books, without being a member of a party" (in Noakes and Pridham, 1983: doc. 93, 138–39).

24. Oranienburg was actually opened by the SA before Dachau, but like other camps it was eventually "nationalized" and given over to the SS under Göring, then to the Gestapo.

Prussia, only about 60 percent of the administrative districts turned in statistics for March and April, but these alone attest to some 16,354 official detentions. Since the reporting districts did not include Berlin, the Reich's capital, plausible calculations for these two months suggest at least 25,000 prisoners *excluding* "wild" detentions (Krausnick et al., 406). By the end of July, even the Ministry of the Interior calculated 26,789 persons in "protective custody" throughout the Reich (Krausnick et al., 410). When prisoners were released—and this could be at any time, since all legal limits on the period of confinement and means of legal recourse had been removed—they were subject to continuous surveillance. As Göring cynically put it, "Those who have begun to be reeducated in the concentration camps need to feel, upon their release, that they have not been left to their own devices. I expect local associations to be conscious of their responsibility as organs of the National Socialist State, and not to abandon these former detainees" (in Wormser-Migot, 63).

The destruction of the German workers' movement was arguably the most spectacular example of *Gleichschaltung,* or "coordination," a key policy of the Nazi government that extended to all spheres of social and political life. Yet, even more disturbing than *Gleichschaltung* was the haste with which many of Germany's elites performed their *Selbst-Gleichschaltung.* This "self-coordination," a bringing of oneself into line, happened at all levels: in the universities and among clergymen, artists, writers, scientists, and doctors. It is acerbically chronicled in Klaus Mann's novel *The Turning Point,* one of many fictional and nonfictional accounts that denounce what Fritz Stern characterizes as a "voluntary, preemptive acceptance of the conformity ordered or expected by the regime," despite the fact that in the opening weeks of the dictatorship "the possibility of cautious criticism still existed without the price of martyrdom" (169). Indeed, Stern provides an impressive list of acts of protest that resulted in no immediately unfavorable consequences for those responsible. The fact that there were not more of these surprised and emboldened Hitler.

Of course, some intellectuals opposed Nazism resolutely, but even they had inner doubts and prejudices to overcome. Thomas Mann's diaries, for example, show him to be completely lucid about the sham behind the Nazis' claim to have led a "people's victory," or a "Brown Revolution." In May 1933 Mann wrote to Albert Einstein: "It is my deepest conviction that this whole 'German Revolution' is indeed wrong and evil. It lacks all the characteristics which have won the sympathy of the world for genuine revolutions, however bloody they may have been. In its essence it is not a 'rising,' no matter how its proponents rant on, but a terrible fall into hatred, vengeance, lust for killing, and petit-bourgeois mean-spiritedness" (1971:198). Yet, even Mann's repugnance for Nazi anti-Semitism does not eschew engrained racialist constructs: "I could to some extent go along with the rebellion against the Jewish element, were it not that the Jewish spirit exercises a necessary control over the German element," he muses (1971:153).

Many of Germany's most renowned personalities joined Mann in exile. While most Western European countries, as well as the United States and Canada, balked at receiving refugees, exceptions were made for "great minds" and "geniuses." Indeed, a new provision of U.S. immigration law introduced specifically for this purpose allowed many prominent German intellectual, scientific, and cultural figures to find a home in America. Among the many more who stayed in Germany, however, the "temptation" of Nazism produced particularly ambivalent feelings. "There were shifting loyalties, admiration for the regime's decisiveness and successes, misgivings about its excesses, careerism, gratification at having others act out one's aggressive or resentful feelings. There was indecision, equivocation, evasion. . . . For most the appeal to German nationalism and the sense of renewed power and purpose reawakened old hopes. Germans were once again a nation to be reckoned with" (Stern, 171).

Anti-Semitism at the Dawn of the Third Reich

The newly won self-esteem of many willing participants in *Selbst-Gleich-schaltung* was intimately bound up with an equally new and unprecedented license to engage in anti-Semitic attitudes and practices. Accused by the Nazis of being ungrateful for the "hospitality" they had received on German soil, Jews were named as among the prime conspirators (along with Bolsheviks and the Allied powers) in Germany's fall. They were seen as "taking up too much space," and the Nazis promised to rid the country of their "corrosive" influence. For the Nazis, who sought to divide Germany into radically distinct camps of *Volksgenossen* (national comrades) and *Gemeinschaftsfremde* (community aliens), Jews were the most alien of all, even though the often unspeakably violent process of forging the *Volk* led to the isolation and persecution of successive groups of designated "aliens" including the mentally ill, the physically handicapped, Romani (Gypsies), Jehovah's Witnesses, homosexuals, insufficiently fertile women, recalcitrant youth, and "welfare bums."

In April 1933, four significant anti-Jewish laws were proclaimed, the first of some four hundred pieces of such legislation promulgated between 1933 and 1939. On April 7, restrictions were placed on Jews in the civil service and the legal profession; on April 22, these were extended to Jewish doctors practicing within the National Health System (NHS); and on April 25, restrictive policies regarding Jewish teachers and quotas for Jewish students were established. While Jews were prohibited from the civil service and from practicing as doctors and lawyers, the exceptions allowed at President von Hindenburg's insistence were significant, since they included all those who had assumed these functions prior to the Weimar period and all Jewish war veterans. As a result, fewer than half of the non-Aryan judges and prosecuting attorneys and only a quarter of the Jewish doctors in the NHS were excludable; the number of Jews in the civil service had been small to begin with (Schleunes, 109). In the case of doctors, many were retained for a time despite the new policy because hospitals required their services. These laws, moreover, followed the largely unsuccessful April boycott of Jewish businesses, which Goebbels had succeeded in whittling down to a single day, April 1, when it became apparent that the original plan for a month-long boycott would meet with international condemnation. Isherwood reports that the boycott was indifferently met in Berlin,[25] although in many smaller towns those who persisted in shopping at "Jewish" businesses were marked with ink stamps on their foreheads and cheeks.[26] The widespread indifference in the capital, as Isherwood perceptively notes, typified a dangerous and generalized abdication of individual responsibility. In the

---

25. Karl A. Schleunes's account in *The Twisted Road to Auschwitz* is more nuanced: "Lack of public enthusiasm for the boycott was particularly disappointing to the Nazis. This apathy may have been the most characteristic response, but there were enough incidents of resistance and expressions of sympathy from German friends to soften the impact for many Jews. . . . Many Jewish shop owners, especially those in working class districts, noted that people were making a point of buying in their store that day" (Schleunes, 88–89).

26. Thirty-two percent of Germany's 500,000 Jews lived in Berlin; only 15% lived in towns with fewer than 10,000 residents (Schleunes, 387).

weeks following the suspension of parliamentary rule, "there were loud-speakers blaring forth speeches by Goering and Goebbels. 'Germany is awake,' they said. People sat in front of the cafés listening to them—cowlike, vaguely curious, complacent, accepting what had happened but not the responsibility for it. Many of them hadn't even voted—how could they be responsible?" (1976: 96).

The boycott also threatened to scare off foreign investors and compromise the well-being of German banks, which had large investments in "Jewish" businesses, especially the major department stores. Despite long-standing Nazi propaganda against these stores and their supposed assault on the small businesses of *Völkisch* merchants, it is significant that no major initiatives were taken against them in the first years of the regime. All these "half measures" disappointed the impatient, chafing legions of the SA, who, along with columnists in the *Völkischer Beobachter*, the Nazi party news-paper, publicly criticized them. In fact, these early laws quickly proved to be incommensurate with the purgative prescribed by Nazi ideologues. In the first place, the laws targeted relatively small segments of the Jewish population—there were approximately 3,000 Jewish lawyers and 5,500 Jewish doctors, and a mere 200 Jewish university teachers in Germany.[27] The limited results achieved by the laws and boycott tended to counter the general theme of the enormity of the "Jewish menace" (in 1933, Jews constituted 0.76 percent of the entire German population, or 503,000 out of a total population of 66,029,000!). More ominously, the laws underscored the more troubling problems of determining who exactly was Jewish and what constituted a "Jewish" business. Between 1910 and 1929, intermarriage between Jews and non-Jews rose from 8 to 23 percent. Many Germans had some Jewish ancestry, and business was hardly organized along ethnic lines, especially when it came to credit and investments! As Schleunes correctly notes, these laws were bound to disappoint the party base precisely because they did *not* "comprise a frontal attack on the blood aspects of assimilation," nor did they address the "biological" issues of race separation (102). The party leadership would stay its hand in this regard until the promulgation of the infamous Nuremberg Laws of September 1935 on Jewish-Aryan relations.

27. All the statistics that follow come from tables and data in Schleunes. Other useful sources in this regard are Krausnick et al., *Anatomy of the SS State;* and Noakes and Pridham, *Nazism 1919–1945: A History in Documents and Eyewitness Accounts.*

Guérin's interview with a well-to-do Jewish family suggests how hard it must have been for such people to believe that a "bohemian corporal" from Austria could make life unlivable, and ultimately lethal, for families that had been in Germany for hundreds of years. Almost all German Jews knew some "Aryans" who seemed to offer reassurance that Hitler's anti-Semitic ravings would not go very far. Certainly the reluctance to abandon business concerns played some role, and Hitler's success in "cutting through" working-class political power would not necessarily have been objectionable to Jewish capitalists any more than to "German" ones. Stern points out that German Jews were often annoyed or embarrassed by their Eastern correligionists' "excessive" dress or observance, their gestures and "voluble" conversation; they sometimes accepted this stereotype of the "Eastern" Jew as much as other Germans did. Perhaps some believed that relations among "respectable" people could be maintained despite Hitler's ravings and the "excesses" of the SA. And so, even though some 37,000 Jews left Germany in 1933 following Hitler's rise,[28] the number fell to 23,000 in 1934, when, in Schleunes's words, "very few measures of public significance were taken against the Jew" (116). Hitler's June 30, 1934, purge of the SA (the Night of the Long Knives) also gave many false hope that the Führer would contain his "unruly" elements. As a result, some 10,000 of those who had fled began to return in the early months of 1935! In fact, most of the Jews who left Germany did so in 1938, many in the wake of the Kristallnacht, when synagogues across Germany were set ablaze and Jewish shops had their windows smashed.[29]

Resistance and the Character of Nazism

The Brown Plague is particularly noteworthy for the prominence it gives to anti-Nazi resistance in 1933. These accounts may at first seem surprising,

28. The right-wing memoirist Robert Brasillach, witnessing the arrival of the first Jewish refugees in Lyon, noted with satisfaction that they appeared to be well-off, and therefore "not persecuted." Clearly, the press had blown their suffering way out of proportion! For him this was confirmed by a final irony: It was a Jew who taught him the "Horst Wessel Lied," the Nazi anthem! (118–19). Anti-Semitism pervades Brasillach's memoir; it is woven integrally into the very fabric of the account. Here, Jews are a recognizable type, wily and disloyal, a foreign body on French soil.

29. Peukert shows that Gestapo reports after the Kristallnacht note popular dissatisfaction at the "needless destruction" of merchandise in Jewish stores when it could have been dis-

since popular histories tend to portray the Nazis' ascension to power as a seamless, monolithic process. As a revolutionary socialist, Guérin was committed to seeking out contacts that could afford him some glimpses into resistance activities, almost all of them dangerous and necessarily clandestine. This active resistance was largely working class in origin, and in the wake of the vast terror and dismantling of legal organizations undertaken during the first few months of the Nazi regime, largely improvised. In some cases, feelings of betrayal led to a refusal to accept centralized leadership; in others, an obstinate belief remained that the party line had been, and continued to be, "correct." But the novelty of the situation as presented by Guérin lies in the efforts of base-level militants to forge new alliances that crossed old party lines. In some cases, older militants had been eliminated by the Nazis, while in others they had been discredited in the eyes of younger militants trying to develop a common strategy.

In Guérin's accounts there are examples of both "noncompliance" and "resistance." The terms are Peukert's, and the distinction is a useful one. In the first case, "the lack of enthusiasm for the character and policies of the regime, and the lack of zeal in the workplace, went along with a retreat into privacy and into the atmosphere of solidarity in small, intimate groups within the working-class social environment" (110). According to the Gestapo's own reports, workers regularly "grumbled" about price increases, privileges at the top, and infringement on their religious rights. Indeed, in the 1934 referendum acclaiming Hitler as Führer, about 25 percent of the voters refused to vote yes, with refusal rates particularly high in Catholic working-class districts.

On the other hand, the depth and breadth of the terror undermined the possibilities of open mass resistance. Peukert notes that "the image of the resistance fighter able to move through his environment like a fish in water is quite inappropriate to the Germany of 1933. The 'water' was being constantly trawled" (105). Militants themselves were often reluctant to reach this conclusion, as evidenced both in the bravado recorded by Guérin in some of his interviews and in the more extensive testimony of other

---

tributed to "Aryans" instead! Others disapproved of the "mob behavior" but saw in it a sad, but acceptable, price to pay when compared with the regime's domestic and international "successes" (58).

resisters.[30] Guérin's second trip to Germany occurred precisely during a period of improvised and often wily attempts to rally workers against the regime. Within the next couple of years, all organized resistance would be smashed, and actions designed to immediately damage the Nazi regime would give way to more modest efforts to preserve class traditions and cohesion while devising plans for a postfascist state.[31] Guérin was fortunate to have known some of these resisters, and more recent research vindicates his determination to present them to a French antifascist readership that, when looking toward Germany in 1933, was all too predisposed to confirm its indiscriminate, smug loathing of the barbaric Boche.

Guérin, however, is always at pains not to confuse "German-ness" with fascism. He constantly evokes scenes from "the other Germany" that he had come to admire as a youth and that stubbornly persisted even under the shadow of Nazism. Guérin believed, as Lord Marley declares in his introduction to the *Brown Book,* that the fight against fascism was not directed *against* Germany; rather, it was a fight "on behalf of the real Germany" (10). Indeed, this was a Germany that Erika Mann could still recognize six years later as Europe prepared to go to war. At the conclusion to *School for Barbarians* (1939), her study of the Nazi indoctrination of children, she bears witness to "voices [that] find the outside world. They are the voices of young workers, students, men of deep religious convictions, and their expressions are of wrath and hope. Here is the spectacle of a country . . . whose moral and spiritual resources are now forced underground. The forces still live. In the past, they nourished all the greatness of Germany. They survive; they cannot be withheld from the soul of a people; they are the highest concepts of human life, and in the end, they triumph" (E. Mann, 154).

La Peste brune *and Its Readers*

Guérin's attitude to his readership in France is above all a didactic one. His conviction that fascism is "essentially aggressive" underpins the urgency

30. For further testimony of resisters, see Peukert (120–23); also Noakes and Pridham (1983: 568–98).

31. Peukert's view of the *active* resistance is that "it was only a minority affair" that "mobilised tens of thousands of people into performing acts of courage and sacrifice, but it

with which he wants to convey its horrors and yet somehow posit its vulnerability to French readers. As a socialist militant, Guérin regards European history in "class-against-class" terms that supersede national interests. Not only does he want to demonstrate that fascism is not an inevitable "German" result, but that the French ruling class and its political and military elites played no small part in contributing to the conditions that made it possible. He reminds his readers that French intervention through the terms dictated by the Treaty of Versailles and the military occupation of the Ruhr Valley had been particularly egregious, exacerbating Germany's economic disaster and making it easier for the Nazis to disparage the young republican traditions established there. Just as Guérin wants to convince French workers that such chauvinistic policies actually work against their interests, his most virulent criticisms of the Social Democrats in Germany are reserved for the occasions when they fall prey to the "logic" of national interest. As for the German Communists, their concessions to German nationalism inevitably prove self-defeating and do nothing to advance the struggle against capital. Ultimately, they serve only to legitimate the propaganda of the Nazis, who are much more at home with this nationalist vision in any case.

Guérin does not embrace the Stalinist view of fascist dictatorship as a conspiratorial objective toward which international capital had been inexorably moving out of economic necessity since the imperialist Great War of 1914–18. Instead, he tends to emphasize its political significance as the full flowering of the terrible violence of a pan-European counterrevolution. If he also allows that fascism is an "emergency response" to the economic crisis made possible by the default of working-class political leadership, he never succumbs to the temptation to see Nazism as a *functional* solution, thus avoiding what Peukert characterizes as a tendency by many analysts to be "taken in by the self-image of National Socialism created by its own propaganda" (44). In fact, Guérin is particularly meticulous in taking apart this propaganda and exposing the very inconsistencies and deceptions that gave it its formidable resiliency in a conjuncture of despair. Guérin is not only writing with the disarray and factionalism of the French workers' movement at the back of his mind; he also knows too well that France has

---

remained decentralised, disoriented, and historically ineffectual. The true historical significance of the resistance was its preservation of non-fascist traditions" (246–47).

many admirers of the German and Italian "experiments" in restoring "purpose" and "order" to life. His aim is to strip away the triumphalist prose of Nazism and reveal the bloodied body of the worker, the Jew, the "marginal" beneath.

The Brown Plague is written in a highly textured and resonant language that bears the distinctive mark of its period. A contemporary reader may marvel at the stark assertion of class over national solidarities that underpins Guérin's analysis, especially when set against the complex realignment of class and national dynamics in the world today, not to mention our reluctance to embrace any "master narrative" of social or political evolution. Striking in this regard are the text's figures of heroic class conflict and the way each section of the 1933 account concludes on an optimistic, if not outright triumphant, note. It is as if each time, Guérin wrestles his own sense of foreboding to the ground in order to rouse French workers from their lethargy and offer them a reason to fight. It seems wholly appropriate to retain this tone in the translation, even at the risk of underscoring how the narrative, for all its intent to create a feeling of immediacy, cannot help but be marked for us by distance. Yet these stylistic features do more than confer upon *The Brown Plague* its unique flavor within the body of eyewitness accounts of Nazism's rise; retaining them and eschewing "modernization" of the text allows a contemporary reader to better appreciate the political and historical culture to which Guérin was heir and that has been largely lost since the Second World War. In particular, Guérin's fondness for employing references to antiquity and European literature to evoke or illustrate aspects of the crisis he depicts may seem surprising to contemporary readers; but far from being unusual or arcane, such references are common in socialist literature of the "classical period," when class struggle was considered worthy of figuration in nothing less than epic terms![32]

Finally, to read Guérin is to avail oneself of a precious opportunity to

32. The discussion of German institutions and personalities in the text assumes at least a general knowledge of them on the part of readers. When Guérin feels elucidation is required, he offers comparisons to equivalent or similar institutions and homologous figures in France. Since these comparisons are likely to be of little assistance to the contemporary English-language reader, I have supplemented the text with a chronology, glossary, and explanatory notes that will provide necessary background in these potentially problematic areas.

understand how the world was imaginatively structured through the militant language of the European Left at mid-century. The polarizations of Guérin's text flow from a conviction that an eschatological choice faced the Western world, and his stylistic choices are based on an evaluation of what kind of language was required to move people politically. In this regard, it is helpful to remember that throughout his youth, Guérin published poetry and fiction that brought letters of encouragement from writers such as Colette and François Mauriac, and that he was received regularly in several of Paris's literary salons. At the age of fourteen, he had announced to his parents that "real life" was to be found in literature, a passion he never abandoned. Yet, as the Brown plague prepared to devour Europe, "real life" directed Guérin's pen toward the monstrous spectacle before his eyes.

1932

February 25	German citizenship is granted to Hitler.
March 13	First round of presidential elections; Hitler receives 13.7 million votes.
April 10	Hindenburg is reelected president in a runoff election.
April 14	The SA and SS are banned by Chancellor Heinrich Brüning.
May 30	Brüning resigns as chancellor.
June 1	Franz von Papen is appointed chancellor.
June 16	The ban on the SA and the SS is lifted by Papen.
July 20	The SPD government in Prussia is removed from office by Chancellor von Papen in the Preussenschlag (Prussian coup).
July 31	Reichstag elections; Nazis win 230 out of 608 seats.
August 9	*Daniel Guérin and companion leave for Germany.*
August 13	Hitler refuses cabinet post offered him by Hindenburg.
September 12	Speaker Göring ignores Chancellor von Papen's attempt to dissolve the Reichstag. Göring's maneuver is nullified, however, and von Papen calls new elections.
November 6	Nazis elect 196 deputies to the Reichstag.
December 3	General Kurt von Schleicher is appointed chancellor.

1933

January 28	Chancellor von Schleicher resigns.

January 30	Hindenburg appoints Hitler chancellor.
February 4	Decree to Protect the German *Volk,* which expands the powers of the police to take people into "protective custody," is announced.
February 22	Approximately 40,000 SA and SS men are sworn in as auxiliary police.
February 27	The Reichstag is burned.
February 28	Hitler is given emergency powers by the Decree of the Reich President for Protecting the *Volk* and the State.
March 5	Reichstag elections; Nazis win 288 seats.
March 13	Joseph Goebbels is appointed Reich minister of public enlightenment and propaganda.
March 21	Communist deputies are forbidden to take seats in the new Reichstag. Special courts are established for the prosecution of political enemies.
March 23/24	Adoption of the Enabling Act. Hitler is allowed to rule for four years without submitting laws for parliamentary approval.
April 1	National boycott of Jewish businesses and professionals.
April 7	Promulgation of the Berufsbeamtengesetz (Civil Service Law), which authorizes the dismissal of Jewish and politically suspect civil servants. This is the first of four anti-Jewish measures adopted during the month of April.
April 26	The Gestapo is formed.
April 30(?)	*Daniel Guérin sets out for his second tour of Germany.*
May 2	Takeover of the labor unions and their "coordination" into the German Labor Front.
May 6–7	Magnus Hirschfeld's Sexual Science Institute is destroyed.
May 10	Book burnings are held throughout Germany, including contents of the Hirschfeld Institute in Berlin. The property of the Social Democratic party, the Reichsbanner, and their press are confiscated.
May 17	Strikes are prohibited. The Reichstag, including the SPD, approves Hitler's foreign policy speech.
May 27	Formal order confiscating property of Communist

	party and press (actually accomplished months earlier) is announced.
June 23	Social Democratic party activities are banned.
July 7	Social Democrats are excluded from all parliaments.
July 14	Law Concerning the Formation of New Parties (i.e., the banning of political parties) is passed.
July 20	Concordat signed between the Vatican and the Third Reich.
October 1	The first concentration camp regulations are issued at Dachau.
October 14	Germany withdraws from the League of Nations.
November 12	Reichstag elections; Nazis receive 93 percent of the vote.

BEFORE THE CATASTROPHE

1 9 3 2

■

Translator's Introduction

The first part of *La Peste brune* is the narrative of a walking tour taken by Daniel Guérin and a companion through pre-Hitler Germany in August and September 1932. Upon his return to France, Guérin reported on this trip in a series of articles that appeared in several periodicals: the illustrated magazine *Vu;* the weekly *Monde,* directed by Henri Barbusse; the revolutionary syndicalist journal *La Révolution Prolétarienne;* and the Communist illustrated *Regards.*[1]

The original edition of *La Peste brune a passé par là* focuses exclusively on the 1933 trip. When Guérin was preparing a new edition many years later, he thought of expanding the volume to include the 1932 articles as originally written; however, rereading them led him to reconsider. In the preface to the Maspero edition, upon which this translation is based, he explains: "Sometimes, they are redundant. They lack homogeneity. Occasionally, they stray from the essential topic: the rise of National Socialism. That is why I have chosen to rewrite the narrative of my first trip in autobiographical form with the help of this raw material. Thus, the text you will read has never before been published. It is not found in earlier editions of *La Peste brune.*"

1. *Vu,* founded by Lucien Vogel in 1928, emphasized photography and photojournalism. *Monde* was founded in 1928 by the Communist intellectual Henri Barbusse, who hoped to regroup intellectual fellow travelers around the journal. *La Révolution Prolétarienne* was published by the Left Opposition expelled from the Communist party in 1923–24. *Regards* was a weekly current affairs publication with a pro-Communist orientation.

An asterisk follows the first use of an abbreviation or proper name that appears in the Glossary. *BT* refers to *The Brown Book of Terror; ETR* refers to *The Encyclopedia of the Third Reich* (see the Bibliography).

Source Articles for Before the Catastrophe *(1932)*

"Sur les routes avec la jeunesse allemande," *Vu,* December 7, 1932.

"Retour au Barbare," *Vu,* March 8, 1933.

"Images d'Allemagne," parts 1 and 2; "Deux Ecoles d'Allemagne," parts 1 and 2, *Monde,* October–November 1932.

"Cette lettre sera peut-être la dernière" [lettre reçue d'Allemagne du 28 février 1933], *Monde,* March 11, 1933.

"Schleicher? Hitler? ou Révolution?" *La Révolution Prolétarienne,* October 10, 1932.

"Victorieuse résistance du prolétariat allemand," *La Révolution Prolétarienne,* November 10, 1932.

"A Kuhle Wampe avec les chômeurs révolutionnaires," *Regards,* December 1932.

At the end of August 1932,[2] I decided to undertake an extensive walking tour of Germany, backpacking as is the custom in that nation. My companion and I prepared with great enthusiasm. Below the fortress of Romainville, the Ourcq Canal stretched before us in a straight line. To better train, we would put on our complete hiking uniform: shirt, corduroy shorts, heavy walking boots, and thick wool socks; we loaded up our rucksacks to the considerable weight they would bear during our journey. Maps in hand, we measured out the precise distance of 12.5 kilometers along the banks of the canal. Then, with a smooth and regular pace, holding our heads high, drawing ourselves up and throwing out our chests, we'd cover this distance every day. When we reached our destination, we would perform a military about-face and cover the same number of kilometers in the opposite direction, indifferent to the sun or inclement weather, ready to take on any difficulty.

The evening of August 9, 1932: Finally, it was time to set out. A trucker who covered the Paris-Strasbourg route every night readily agreed to pack us into his "heavy load." The enormous vehicle jolted and clanked on the cobblestones of Pantin. In the trailer, between two rolls of linoleum of an imposing diameter, my companion and I lodged our bruised bodies and our stuffed and misshapen packs topped off by their mess tins. Behind the steering wheel and in the cabin sat a couple of tall, blond, mild-mannered Alsatian boys. From time to time, we joined them for a chat. To get a look

2. This must be a typographical error because in the following paragraph Guérin gives August 9 as the day of departure for the tour. In his archival notes, moreover, Guérin gives August 10 as the date of his arrival in Germany, consistent with the nighttime departure on August 9 he describes.

at the countryside, all we had to do was lift the canvas cover of the trailer. Most of the time, though, we lay sprawled over the rough packages like lazy kings and let the hours slip by. When night finally came and the exhausted drivers made a roadside stop, off we went to a neighboring field and brought back some soft sheafs of freshly cut wheat to cushion the edges and absorb the shocks.

At the edge of the Black Forest, I was overflowing with an optimism not yet shaken by the vicissitudes of the social struggle; an optimism hardly shared by my carefree and skeptical petit-bourgeois companion! After such a long period of sterile inaction in my degenerate old country, perhaps I would finally find myself at the heart of the action in this youthful, modern, and dynamic Germany that I had admired unceasingly since my childhood. It was here that socialism would triumph, or nowhere. It was here that the world's best organized and most educated working class had taken form. Here economic and social contradictions had reached a point of extreme tension. Here the hour would sound when the formidable bloc of wage earners would have it out once and for all with the mercenaries of big capital.

And yet the seeds of a mortal illness were already corrupting this flesh, so resplendent in appearance. Birds flew low in a heavy sky, as if before a storm. The farther I would plunge into the heart of this country, the more disillusioned I would become. The truth was that despite a few misleading appearances here and there, everything was presaging, everything was fomenting—without my yet being fully aware of it—the victory of Hitlerite fascism.

———————

At the end of a fine afternoon, we completed the first segment of our journey beyond the Rhine. Our legs had already carried us twenty-five kilometers, and despite the fact that we had trained for this distance, we felt weighted down by the burdens on our shoulders. We passed through a village that seemed stylish compared with the ones in France, with small, freshly painted white houses, their windows lined with geraniums. Like a horse who smells its stable, we stepped a bit more lightly when, on the other side of the small settlement, off to the side and surrounded by trees, appeared the shelter we'd been seeking: the youth hostel. It would be like this every evening, as if we were coming home.

The common room was already full: youths aged between fifteen and twenty, blond-haired with virile voices and determined faces. Khaki or green sport shirts with rolled-up sleeves revealed their tan forearms. Sculptured knees emerged from corduroy or leather shorts often held up by a pair of Tyrolian suspenders with a wide rectangular patch of leather forming a kind of bridge between the pectorals. Legs were deeply tanned, muscles taut and hard. Thick socks tumbled down to strong, monumental shoes.[3] Some youths gallantly sported tiny, ecclesiastical skullcaps made from gray felt cut out of the bottom of old hats.

We wasted no time in getting acquainted, and the fact that we were French earned us a fraternal welcome.

"Franzose? Impossible! We see Franzosen so rarely."

Then a volley of questions:

"Is there lots of unemployment in your country, too?"

"Is it true what they say, that the French are really rich and have lots of gold?"

"Do you have compulsory military service?"

"What do you call us? . . . Boches?"

We responded as well as we could. Around us, a circle had formed; a circle at the center of which I felt quite at ease. In their faces I read not only a need for direct communication beyond artificial borders, lying newspapers, and speeches, but also their surprise that we were like them.

On a table, the "golden book": each visitor is asked to write his name in it and leave a trace—a thought, a poem, a drawing—of his passage. On the cover page, this unheeded notice: "You are requested to keep your politics out of this book." Yet, as I leafed through it, politics welled up on every page. Politics tormented these youths to the point where they were unable to resist, despite the neutral ambiance of the hostel. One hand had written, "Workers of the world, unite!" But another had obliterated the appeal with a violent stroke of the pen. On another page, the three Socialist arrows pierced a swastika. We were told that these passions were rather recent.

By comparison, when I described the ignorance and indifference of French youth numbed by the opium of the sports newspapers, I was informed that it wasn't so long ago that German youths were far more

---

3. Guérin is referring to the traditional *Lederhosen* (shorts) and *Waldstrümpfe* (socks) worn by hikers.

interested in champions and stars than in Hitler* or "Teddy" Thälmann.*
But unemployment, poverty, and the boisterous arrival of National Socialism on the scene had changed all that. Because they were eighteen years
old, I was still able to read a joie de vivre deep in the faces of my companions that evening, but there was also anguish and hunger. These lux-
uriously appointed hostels, where handsome but unused stoves contrasted
with tightening belts, suggested a fragile world. The contagion of political
fanaticism had spread even to the prepubescent youths. A thirteen-year-old
boy shouted his love of the Führer to me, a young girl discussed with great
seriousness the latest speech of Chancellor von Papen.* The uncommitted
were few; everyone had taken sides.

The common room emptied little by little. At opposite ends, two groups
stayed behind. In the semidarkness, one group of schoolchildren clutched
their song sheets. Under the direction of their schoolmasters they intoned
martial airs about victorious heroes and routed enemies. Three sturdy and
strapping Westphalian youths, undoubtedly proletarians, listened to them
with satisfaction and eventually took up the refrain. At the other end of the
room, other hostelers indisposed by this performance observed mutely and
scowled. One of them held the Communist daily, *Rote Fahne*,[4] in his
clenched fingers. And when I vainly attempted to get him to speak, he
gestured toward the enemy camp with a nod of his head and shrugged his
shoulders. Nazis and revolutionaries would confront each other thus, as if
on the eve of battle, until the time came for "lights out."

A more loquacious—or lucid—youth murmured in my ear as we returned to our dormitory, "You see, we're pitted against each other. Our
passions are so white-hot that occasionally we kill each other, but *deep
down we want the same thing . . ."*

"Really?"

"Yes, *the same thing*, a new world, radically different from today's, a
world that no longer destroys coffee and wheat while millions go hungry, *a
new system*. But some *believe adamantly* that Hitler will provide this, while
others believe it will be Stalin. That's the only difference between us."

And that's why in the barracks, before the lights went out, an old vagabond road song which the Nazi intoned with as much conviction as the Socialist or the Communist would resound from some fifty sonorous breasts:

4. *Red Flag.*

> As we walk along side by side
> And sing the ancient airs
> Which the forests echo back
> Then, we feel, it has to happen:
>
> With us will come new times!
> With us will come new times!

The unanimity was barely shattered by the discord of three antagonistic cries shouted in unison as if to say goodnight or issue a final challenge:

"Heil Hitler!"

"Freiheit!"

"Rotfront!"[5]

And yet the dilettantes and poets, the literary and romantic survivors of the *Jugendbewegung*[6] of the pre–1914 period, had not—as yet—completely disappeared. Take, for example, the group of students we met on the road the following day, simply clad in shorts, practically naked under a leaden sun. An unlikely collection of articles was heaped upon their backs. They could have been taken for a camel caravan transporting merchandise! These happy-go-lucky fellows stubbornly preferred the cult of nature to political controversy. To the accompaniment of a guitar, they quietly sang these lyrics by Hermann Löhne, a poet killed at the front:

> And my heart sings, my heart sings
> An air which rises to heaven, too,
> An air so light and tender,
> An air as delicate and tender
> As a tiny cloud fleeing through the azure
> Like a whisp of down in the breeze . . .

5. "Freiheit" (Freedom!) was the slogan of the Social Democrats; "Rotfront" (Red Front!) that of the Communists. In the original edition, the latter is erroneously transcribed from the German as "Rot Front."

6. "Youth movement"; Guérin is referring to the hiking and camping movements so prevalent in pre–World War I Germany. For additional reading, see Becker (1946), Laqueur (1984), and the German sources cited in note 4 of the Introduction. Before 1914, these movements "promised a total renewal of society through a return to nature and transcendental values. . . . [T]he German youth movement's history is also linked to that of homosexuality" (Steakley, 54).

But in Germany in the summer of 1932, those hostelers who wandered by choice were less numerous than the vagabonds who did so out of necessity. At the very least, half a million jobless youths wandered the roads. They had no right to social assistance, most often because at least one member of their family was still working. Fed up with twiddling their thumbs in their grim working-class neighborhoods and being a burden on their families, they would set out each spring and knock about in the world until autumn's end. Some had been drifting like this for several years, without any goal, living off charity, taking refuge in shelters and stables. In general, they traveled in pairs along the busiest roads, a large cane or walking stick in hand, pillaging fruit trees, practicing what had not yet been baptised hitchhiking. When they formed a group, one would play an instrument while the others, born musicians like all Germans, would sing in chorus. Some were jokers and fatalistic, others even cynical and servile: if you want to eat, you have to know how not to displease people. The day would come (and we didn't yet know how close that day was) when the latter would sell themselves to the highest bidder; or else their resentments, having accumulated for too long, would explode with brutality, their blows raining down freely on the scapegoats that had been designated for them.

On the banks of a river where we were bathing, we met a couple of buddies. One—when he had work—was a shoemaker; the other was a dyer. Today, they had nothing to clothe themselves with but patched-up vests under which they were bare-chested; laughing, they showed us their worn-out boots, their long, pink toes poking out the ends and taking the air. Out of a torn pocket they carefully removed a soiled booklet, their official "nomad book." Page after page of place-names, inscribed in ink or pencil, stamps affixed. Some names already reappeared two or three times and would doubtless appear again on pages that were still blank. A hellish cycle. It would end only when they enrolled in the Brownshirts[7] or were taken on by an armaments factory.

But while waiting, the prefascist government had already scooped up some of these tramps as "volunteers" for militarized labor camps. To die of hunger or consent to being thus "enrolled": that was the alternative for German youth in 1932.

From the bridge at Kehl to our arrival in Saxony, a long journey traveled

---

7. The familiar name for Storm Troopers (SA).

sometimes on foot and sometimes by train, we had a dominant impression: the population had already shifted to the side of the Nazis. The epidemic was widespread, and it was ravaging city and countryside alike.

In every village square a tall, insolent pole visible from afar bore an enormous red standard—a screaming red—scored with the black swastika. On the walls of the town hall or the schools were notice boards to which the pages of the National Socialist daily were affixed. On the tables of the beer halls, set in luxurious bindings, lay the party magazines.

I entered a peasant's home to buy eggs and milk. Portraits of the Führer cut out of some illustrated magazine were crudely mounted on the walls.

"Our savior!" proclaimed the father, with an opaque certainty.

They spread out before me a pile of Hitlerite tracts amassed during the last electoral campaign. They came in all shapes, sizes, and colors. The son declared in a rough voice which neither allowed nor even could imagine contradiction: "The National Socialist list won an absolute majority here!"[8]

Meanwhile the mother was hunting feverishly through a cupboard. Finally she extracted a cigar box from its hiding place and presented it to me. I protested that I wasn't a smoker. Then she opened it and pulled out a wad of yellowed bank notes and shouted, while her son gazed stonily at me: "All of our assets! Everything we saved during twenty years of working like slaves. Now, it's worth nothing . . . not a pfennig, sir! The Social Democrats, with *their* inflation, have taken it all."

In the cities, the young SA's* took over the sidewalks and paraded about in their brand-new overwaxed boots and shoulder straps. Around the Brown Houses, guarded by numerous sentries, there prevailed an intense commotion of comings and goings amidst crowds of onlookers and sympathizers. Inside was a state within a state that was already the embryo of a new state.

It was in Rothenburg, a small medieval Bavarian city so well preserved

8. In the elections of July 31, 1932, held shortly before Guérin's arrival in Germany, only one district out of thirty-five (Schleswig-Holstein) gave the Nazis an absolute majority, with 51% of the vote. In the last free elections of November 6, the Nazis failed to win an absolute majority anywhere. In the larger cities, their totals were 22.5% in Berlin, 27.2% in Hamburg, 17.4% in Cologne-Aachen, 34% in Dresden-Bautzen, 25.6% in Dusseldorf, 18.5% in Lower Bavaria including Munich, 31% in Leipzig. In general, the Nazis fared better in smaller population centers.

that it seemed to be made out of cardboard, that I had my first conversation with a Nazi militiaman. Heated, speaking at the top of his voice, eyes bloodshot, but with an entirely Germanic courtesy he opened his heart to me, as if he had a burning need to unburden it.

A fanatical petit-bourgeois taxi driver who drove his own car, he explained that he had belonged to the Social Democratic party for a long time but finally quit in disgust. He reproached "Marxism" for having betrayed both Germany and the proletariat. Here he was now, head of a Storm Trooper section and an extremist within his new party.

"Will Hitler take part in a coalition?"

"No! No! A thousand times no!" he shouted, as if going on in this manner appeased him. *"All or nothing!"*

The inn where he invited us to have a *bock* served as the local party headquarters. Suddenly, the door flung open with a violent crash, as uniformed motorcyclists, headstrong toughs outfitted in leather boots and caps, burst into the room like a gust of wind. With puerile conviction, our taxi driver and the proprietor of the bar explained how Hitler would put an end to unemployment, get rid of poverty, and usher in a *new system.*

It was the same story in a small village in Franconia, not far from Bayreuth. Here the scene was an open-air swimming pool sheltered by boulders and fir trees. Groups of liberated suntanned bodies relaxed around us. But once again, politics triumphed over nature. Armed with a tiny shovel, naked as a worm, a little boy threw sand in our eyes and stepped over us. He was so handsome, so blond, of such a pure Germanic type that I asked his father for permission to photograph him.

"But of course! You will show the French this portrait of a little German and you will ask them to be less unjust toward his country." Then, the nature worshipper launched into a violent diatribe against the Treaty of Versailles, against imperialist France. Stretched out under the burning sun, eyes closed, hands behind his head, he argued for compulsory military service not to make war, he explained, but to "discipline" youth. Because I attempted to counter him with arguments in which a whiff of "Marxism" was detected, he lashed out at the Social Democratic leaders who, according to him, had spent the previous fourteen years filling their own pockets instead of working for the proletariat.

And suddenly: "Look, answer me frankly: Since you seem to be so interested in the German proletariat, would you really wish a Stalinist regime upon it?"

––––––––––

In my train compartment, I began leafing through a bundle of Communist illustrated papers which I had taken out of my rucksack. With a heavy step, a laborer in work clothes got on the train and occupied the seat next to mine.

Noticing him cast a furtive glance at my newspapers, I offered them to him. He began reading them attentively, one by one, without saying a word. But I had not paid attention to two youths sitting at the other end of the compartment: on their elegantly cut jackets, they wore swastikas. They didn't stir, but surveyed their prey out of the corners of their eyes.

Arriving at his destination, the worker got up and took down the small sack that contained his belongings from the baggage net. One of the two stood up, handed him a *Völkischer Beobachter*,[9] and requested—politely but imperiously—that he take it with him. A second's hesitation, then the man, fearstruck, decided to take the sheet, saluted awkwardly with a tip of his hat, and disappeared.

––––––––––

In a small city where we stopped one afternoon, a children's festival was taking place in the main square. It was an idyllic spectacle. Sons and daughters of workers, heads adorned with floral wreaths, were dancing in a circle and singing in chorus with crystal-clear voices. I whispered to my companion, "This must be a workers' celebration."

He frowned skeptically, and not without cause. In fact, we met these same children again at nightfall, swarms of them in the streets, on their way home. They were led by their parents, proletarians dressed in their Sunday best. Each tyke proudly carried a stick from which hung a glowing colored lantern on which a swastika had been emblazoned in bold black strokes.

––––––––––

Nevertheless, in the industrial centers we were to meet some Reds. One

9. The official newspaper of the Nazi party.

Sunday we arrived at a large town near Stuttgart to empty streets, Sunday boredom, the sound of hymns, and the ringing of church bells. Suddenly the "Internationale"[10] startled me. My companion smiled at my emotion. I stopped in my tracks like a hunting dog, sniffing, seeking out the song's source. The sound led us to the back room of a beer hall, where young boys and girls welcomed us warmly with clenched fists and "Rotfront's." They belonged to a proletarian sports club in Stuttgart, and since they were on their way home after a Sunday excursion, they invited us to come along in their pick-up truck. The girls had bobbed hair and browned arms that could have been men's. The boys in their shorts, as virile as one could hope for, resembled the revolutionaries one sees in historical murals.

On the trip through the interminable working-class districts of Stuttgart, they went through the entire repertory of Communist songs, provoking enthusiasm everywhere. Families out for a walk, lovers out on the town, women on their doorsteps, toddlers in the gutters, friendly cyclists with garlanded handlebars—with faces aglow, all raised their fists and shouted enthusiastically "Rotfront!"

I felt better. My confidence returned. I felt a physical sensation of being gripped by what I believed to be the power of the revolutionary German proletariat.

But most often the trade union movement presented a much less comforting spectacle, especially in the large cities. Take, for example, the People's House in Dresden. "House" is really an understatement. Before us stood a colossal building, the work of an up-to-the-minute architect.

First we entered the beer hall with its heavy armchairs. Beneath our hiking boots, of which we were suddenly ashamed, a thick carpet muffled our step: the silent and coddled atmosphere of an expensive club. A headwaiter in an elegant white jacket approached, obsequious at first. But our apparel, so unusual in this plush place, produced a rather ironic inflection in his voice. He presented us with the menu: a long list of refined dishes, at prices obviously beyond the reach of working-class budgets. At a neighboring table, two or three heavy drinkers were deeply involved in an intense card game, downing large *bocks* and banging the table loudly with their fists.

10. The revolutionary anthem composed during the Paris commune.

Suddenly, the word *bonze*,[11] the name Communists and Nazis commonly called the reformist leaders, took on its full meaning for me. Our neighbors the card players were *bonzes*, and we had fallen into their lair. They were gallant men, for all that. Learning that we were French comrades, they cordially invited us to join them in their libations. Red in the face, bloated, and dull, confined to their cushy, tiny, bureaucratic and corporative world, they made me want to grab them by the collar and give them a good shaking. Seven or eight million German proletarians were dying of hunger and millions of others were working with half-empty bellies. The fascist peril was at the door. But the *bonzes* of Dresden treated themselves to a good time.

They had the courtesy to give us a tour of this People's House[12] which no longer belonged to the people, and we soon found ourselves in elevators driven by perpetual motion. One would catch them in flight and alight without disturbing their noiseless coming and going. In a single bound, we reached the summit: a rooftop garden where, caught unprepared, we stood before the immense city glistening in the sun.

We were spared nothing, neither the well-lit meeting rooms, decorated in lively and audacious colors, where trade unionists, as if made uneasy by the ambiance, maintained a stiff silence; nor the hotel rooms, furnished in costly Louis XV style, that on rare occasions were made available to Social Democratic parliamentarians on propaganda tours.

I rubbed my eyes. Had the revolution already happened? Certainly not, for behind this showy palace were millions of people without bread or hope and others who were planning to rob the working class of its final conquests. The old world was disintegrating. The time had come to risk everything. Yet the noise of battle did not penetrate these walls; it was muffled by this soundproofed luxury.

The People's House in Dresden was the symbol and the product of a

11. Literally, a Buddhist monk of China or Japan. Used pejoratively to describe the parasitic and privileged lives led by the Social Democratic trade union leadership.
12. These institutions were organically linked to the Social Democratic party in Germany. Their French equivalent, the *bourses du travail* (labor exchanges), were not affiliated with a political party and were usually more modest, although some were built with municipal subsidies. Originating in the 1880s, they federated to form the CGT* in 1895. Union meetings would take place there (these were prohibited on work sites in France until 1936) as well as social occasions, weddings, and lectures.

collective folly. All Germany had lost its head over American-style delusions of grandeur. While the captains of industry built factories three times more beautiful and with a productive capacity three times larger than required, while municipalities and public administrations erected train stations, post offices, and youth hostels, all on a gargantuan scale, the trade union *bonzes,* not to be outdone, squandered their members' dues on luxurious buildings. But these houses didn't prevent workers' wages from melting away during the economic crisis; and at a time when they should have been coming to grips with the Brownshirts, this luxury emasculated the leaders who had grown sluggish from the delights of Capoua.[13]

When I risked expressing my discomfort, albeit in guarded terms, my guide explained with lyrical obstinacy: "We want our leaders to have beautiful, well-furnished offices because they are *our* leaders. Each worker is proud that the organized working class has been able to achieve such marvels. After visiting our beautiful People's House, he leaves with the idea of improving his condition . . ."

I could no longer contain myself: "Don't you rather think that from that moment on he will have but one thought: in order to live better, he should become a *bonze* himself?"

Without doubt, never had such nonconformist language troubled the quietude of this bureaucrat. In vain, he sought a response.

"And tell me, if the Brownshirts one day invade your People's House, how will you defend yourselves?"

"If . . . ? What are you saying? If the . . . ?"

He knew by heart how much had been spent on the telephones that were deployed like accordions, the metal filing cabinets, and the office chairs that were so deep that one lost all sense of time in them. But this . . . no, really, he had never thought about it.

As for the Communists, they had already written off this entire reformist apparatus and surrendered it in their minds to Hitler. A tall, thin boy with an orthodox and inquisitorial look stared at me from the top of his 6′4″ frame and confided: "It's all the same to us if the Nazis get their hands on those palaces and those *bonzes* . . . For our part, we have nothing to lose.

---

13. A reference to the place where Hannibal's troops rested too long and were caught unprepared and routed.

On the contrary! We Communists will work much better under illegal conditions than legal ones."

Tomorrow, shrewd marauders, taking advantage of the people's disarray and indifference, would lay claim to these riches without firing a shot. And in the palaces, they would replace the overthrown *bonzes* with their own.[14]

That very evening in Dresden, National Socialism paraded its growing strength before us. It began in the afternoon with a squadron of airplanes passing swiftly and noisily over the city, swooping down to release a rain of small leaflets, then soaring upward again in combat formation. On the roads that converge on the Saxonian capital, there was a parade of Nazis on foot, on bicycle, and in trucks, all flocking in from the surrounding villages. Petit-bourgeois elements dominated the crowd that was waiting in the bleachers of the immense sports stadium. First of all, an interminable military parade: In the faint glimmer of the spotlights, to the din of a despairingly banal music, the Storm Trooper sections advanced one by one, flags at the head of their formations. When the pace slowed, they stamped mechanically in the dust, keeping time with swinging arms.

With the passing of each standard, ten thousand arms rose and gave the Roman salute. And this took place twenty-five times in a row. After having gone completely around the stadium, each section arranged itself in a square formation at the center of the field around a grandstand set up for the speakers. Before us extended a sea of Brownshirts standing at attention.

Finally, the long-awaited leader appeared. Bareheaded and surrounded by bodyguards, he was greeted by enthusiastic "Heils." Outfitted in boots and belt, with a black tie over his brown shirt, he was stubby-legged, bald, slightly obese, with a protruding lower lip. Gregor Strasser* looked more grotesque than soldierlike. In "civilian life" he was a pharmacist, and the panoply in which he was rigged out failed to camouflage his vulgar petit-bourgeois bearing. But he was hardly a fool. He was reputed to be one of the most gifted and furthest to the "left" of all the Nazi leaders. Some even claimed that he was the real leader of the party. In fact, his strong person-

---

14. This anticipates "The Swastika over the Trade Unions," the tenth chapter of Guérin's 1933 narrative.

ality overshadowed Hitler's, who would have him slain like a dog on June 30, 1934.

For two hours the loudspeakers brought us tirades of highly eloquent demagogy with a strength of conviction that one would be foolish to underestimate: "The essential truth of our time is that 90 percent of the German population believes the capitalist system has outlived itself and demands something else . . . a new economy . . . a new system . . ." (Shouts from all over, "Yes, that's it . . . *Jawohl!*"). Then, as one voice, the immense choir sang out the "Horst Wessel Lied"*[15] in an élan of collective hypnosis.

When we arrived in Berlin on September 5, with that slight tingling of the spine that accompanies the discovery of a great capital, we experienced a change of scene that was as abrupt as it was unexpected.

In fact, Berlin might have been taken for a great garrison town in which all the troops had been given leave from their barracks at once. In contrast to the youthful SA, this soldiery bore the stigmata of age. Were these the "territorials," as we called them in France, these fat men with monumental buttocks, redundant bellies, and shabby uniforms? When they took off their green caps (an abominable green), the sweat from their polished, boulderlike skulls overflowed into their checkered handkerchiefs. They wandered about in tight groups, taking up the entire width of the sidewalk, having themselves photographed at the foot of the colossal equestrian monument to Wilhelm I, and gathering under the neoclassical cupola that sheltered the Unknown Soldier. The golden eyeglasses of Herr Doktor alternated with the monocle of the Junker,[16] while legions of peasants, still half serfs, dragged along in heavy boots. The aristocratic haughtiness of some alternated with the thundering vulgarity of others.

Out of what trapdoor had this old military and imperial Germany loomed up? It had been brought back to life in the space of a morning through the will of Chancellor von Papen. These gentry of the *ancien régime*—squires, generals, industrialists, barons of the Herrenklub[17]—were not without mixed feelings toward the plebian gangs of Adolf Hitler. They fancied that they would be able to counterbalance the ruffians by means of

15. The anthem of the Nazi party. See Glossary, Horst Wessel.
16. Literally, the Prussian landed aristocracy. As an epithet in more general usage, it suggests arrogance, narrow-mindedness, and authoritarianism.
17. An influential association of politicians, bankers, big employers, big landowners, high-ranking civil servants, and officers.

their more sober cohorts, steeped in venerable Prussian discipline. If it came right down to it, they would agree to share power with this parvenu who had started off as a building painter, but they weren't about to hand it over to him. They had other ideas about governing the Reich: if need be, they would surrender a few secondary portfolios to commoners with neither education nor experience, but they would keep the levers of command for themselves.

This is why, on the occasion of their annual congress, they had assembled in the capital, at great expense and from the four corners of the country, over 150,000 veterans of the so-called Stahlhelm[18] organization. Borrowing the National Socialists' propaganda techniques, they hoped to thumb their noses at Hitler through a noisy spectacle and a gigantic parade.

At the hour when the decisive clash between fascism and revolution was expected, what was this specter of a dead past doing on the scene? In any case, whether or not it was merely a historical reenactment or an intermezzo without consequence, the stage director had done a good job.

I found myself a bit too close for comfort to these fat green men. On the platform of a bus, I was squashed between their rotundities, their shoulder straps, and their Iron Crosses. The Stahlhelm were obese, stupid, and crass reactionaries: the narrow-minded petit bourgeois, the hopelessly dense yokel, the out-and-out *revanchard,*[19] the irreversible Reaction.

For a single day, Potsdam, the Versailles of Frederick the Great, came back to life. Flags with imperial colors flew from every window. Old roughnecks had taken their gleaming archaic uniforms out of camphor and arrogantly donned their pointed helmets—the same helmet which I, during my childhood, had drawn with trembling fingers to look like the horns of the devil. In the great park with its towering foliage, these lard-encased troopers offended nature and violated one's sight, hearing, and sense of smell. Beneath the arbors, around the marble pools, they advanced in measured step in tight-knit packs, stopping suddenly on command with a rumbling of clicked heels. Bumpkins with harsh country accents smiled

18. "Steel Helmet"; an association of ex-servicemen founded on December 25, 1918. In the mid-1920s, it had some 400,000 members. The group was antirepublican and favored an authoritarian form of government. Although it facilitated Hitler's seizure of power, it was "absorbed" by the new regime and dissolved in 1935.

19. Those who advocated remilitarization and war in order to avenge the 1919 Treaty of Versailles (Fr. *revanche,* "revenge").

lewdly and pointed at the finely chiseled breasts on the statues. Others, flat on their bellies and in spite of the rucksacks that grotesquely doubled the volume of their backs, amused themselves by trying to catch fish in the pools. Mess trucks with chimneys that looked like they came from pre-historic locomotives were stationed around the periphery of the park, ready to shovel food into all these potbellied men.

Before the tomb of the last empress of Germany (a small antique temple overgrown with ivy and surrounded by a grill), the green men froze with a dry sound: "Swear here to restore Germany to its place above all peoples!" hammered a giant with a severe face and a carnivorous voice.

"We swear it!"

The "gentlemen," however, would be rash to claim victory. If the veterans and a part of the officer corps were on their side, support among the masses and in parliament was rather weak. Thus, they would now try to consolidate their fragile position.

On September 12, 1932, the Reichstag was convened for a meeting that, it was rumored, could well be historic. I didn't want to miss this spectacle, but I would have been denied entry in my "globe-trotter" outfit. An obliging Social Democrat lent me a suit which was much too large and in which I seemed to float. Then, having succeeded in getting a press card, I made a very dignified entrance into the parliamentary palace, arriving by taxi, with a military salute from a row of Schupos.*

Compared with the Palais-Bourbon,[20] the atmosphere on the floor seemed morose to me. Here, individual personalities hardly seemed to count for anything. As the benches slowly filled, one could make out only compact and clearly delineated blocs: each party's parliamentary caucus. Each had its particular tone, as if its members were cast from the same mold.

Here, first of all, majestic in its good manners, was Social Democracy: you would have taken them for drab old professors from the provinces and slightly starchy women of a mature age. It was difficult to imagine that this was once the party of August Bebel* and Wilhelm Liebknecht.*

20. I.e., the edifice housing France's Chamber of Deputies. Today, the Chamber itself is known as the Assemblée nationale, although under the Third Republic this term was reserved for joint meetings of the Chamber and the Senate.

The Communists were younger, more dynamic, the women not as prim but every bit as dignified and attentive. Sitting apart from all the other groups, the eighty-nine representatives of the Third International gave the impression, or at least the illusion, of being a solid block.

Then there were the men of Zentrum, prelates in civilian garb, with black morning coats and clean-shaven, sly expressions; then the hunched-up barons of Hugenburg's Conservative party; and still further to the right, the provocative, plebian, turbulent mass of 230 Hitlerites. Among them were many young men—good-looking, insolent fellows. They didn't yet dare wear their brown shirts to sessions of parliament, but the corridors and vicinity of the Reichstag were swarming with booted militiamen.

In the Speaker's chair, a high Gothic throne, appeared a kind of large, beardless doll with a disturbing jaw—half executioner, half clown. Wearing a chestnut sports jacket with a floppy collar, elegant and impertinent, he seemed to be enjoying himself prodigiously. But when he opened his mouth, the voice that emerged was as vicious as that of the giant I had seen in Potsdam. Glints of ferocity passed through the vacant eyes of this morphine addict.[21] Speaker Hermann Göring* gave the floor to the Communist deputy Torgler.[22] With a few brief, skillful, and violent words, the Stalinist opened the attack against the government. Lined up behind a table to the right of the podium, like in a shooting gallery, the ministers sat unflinching. They looked like the respectable board of some corporation.

Göring, after a brief recess, announced in a cutting tone that the Communists' resolution of no confidence would be put to a vote.[23] Chancellor

21. "[Göring's] biographers tell us of his heroic deeds as an airman during the [First] war. They forget to add that his flights were carried out when he was under the influence of morphia." In April 1926 a Stockholm police doctor certified that Göring was of "unsound mind" and a morphine addict. He was hospitalized but eventually "could no longer be kept in private mental homes because the staff were unwilling to look after him. And in Langbro [asylum], he had such bad attacks that he had to be put into the section for serious cases" (*BT,* 138–43).

22. Ernst Torgler (1893–1963) was the leader of the KPD's caucus in the Reichstag.

23. "Papen, who was aware of the decline in Nazi morale [see Introduction, pp. 18–19 for a discussion of the crisis of the Nazi party in 1932], decided to apply pressure on the Party by calling another election in which he reckoned they would lose votes. . . . On September 12, therefore, he dissolved Parliament. The Nazis could only retaliate rather futilely by holding up the dissolution until a motion of 'no confidence' proposed by the Communists had been passed by 513 votes to thirty-two" (Noakes and Pridham, 1974:136).

von Papen rose, pretentious, disagreeable, and very pale. With a barely visible gesture, he demanded the floor. But the horrible doll in the Speaker's chair turned his head elsewhere and pretended not to see him. The second time, Papen raised his forefinger in a determined manner. In vain. Such a sacrilege had never before been seen in a German parliament. Trembling with contained rage, the chancellor then pulled out a pink portfolio from under his arm. Walking quickly to the Speaker's desk, he handed Göring a small piece of paper and then left the chamber followed by his barons in single file.

The doll caught the paper in flight, tossed it disdainfully to the other side of his desk, and sarcastically announced that the vote on the Communists' resolution would continue.

For the urns were already circulating. When the ballots were counted, the old spectral Germany had received only thirty-three votes. Marxism and fascism had formed a bloc against it.

Suddenly, a tiny, awkward monkey leapt forth from his bench. In two strides he reached the Gothic throne and with volubility and forceful gestures admonished the drug fiend. Duly lectured by Dr. Goebbels,* Göring then proclaimed that the government had been defeated, and that as a consequence the decree dissolving the Reichstag that Papen had taken out of his pink portfolio was null and void.

Rumors swept through Berlin like a burning powder fuse: tomorrow the army would occupy the Reichstag—a professional army of 100,000 men, well-trained after seven years of service, modern, and fully equipped. Would Göring have to play Mirabeau?[24] Would there be a confrontation between the two right-wing camps? In fact, they lost no time in reaching an agreement. An hour after the session, it was learned, Göring backed down and bowed to constitutional legality. The Reichstag, in which the NSDAP* had 230 seats, was dissolved after all. The Hitlerian braggarts didn't dare cross swords with the Reichswehr.[25]

---

24. It was Mirabeau who defied King Louis XVI when he ordered the dissolution of the Estates General. In a turning point of the events leading to the French Revolution, Mirabeau rejected the king's authority to dissolve the sovereign assembly of the nation's representatives. Guérin's sarcastic analogy obviously places Göring, as Speaker of the Reichstag, in Mirabeau's position and Chancellor von Papen in the king's!

25. I.e., the army. See note 16 in the Introduction regarding Hitler's "sacrifice" of the SA to the Reichswehr on the Night of the Long Knives, June 30, 1934.

For a brief moment, the old Germany carried the day. But it desired an open conflict no more than the National Socialists. Rather than joining together, the left-wing parties vainly tried to split apart these two adversarial camps, believing they could outsmart them. Soon, the Third Reich would be born out of the disunity of the proletariat *and* a compromise between the old and new "gentlemen." On September 12, this was already in the air.[26]

One Sunday on the outskirts of Berlin, we met by chance a strange troupe on the road. Needless to say, neither their short pants, their bare calves, which disappeared under their long wool vests, the bulky and sundry loads swaying on their backs, nor their enormous hiking boots distinguished them from ordinary vagabonds. But they were very much "toughs." They had the depraved and troubled faces of hoodlums and the most bizarre coverings on their heads: black or gray Chaplinesque bowlers, old women's hats with the brims turned up in "Amazon" fashion adorned with ostrich plumes and medals, proletarian navigator caps decorated with enormous edelweiss above the visor, handkerchiefs or scarves in screaming colors tied any which way around the neck, bare chests bursting out of open skin vests with broad stripes, arms scored with fantastic or lewd tattoos, ears hung with pendants or enormous rings, leather shorts surmounted by immense triangular belts—also of leather—both daubed with all the colors of the rainbow, esoteric numbers, human profiles, and inscriptions such as *Wild-frei* (wild and free) or *Räuber* (bandits). Around their wrists they wore enormous leather bracelets. In short, they were a bizarre mixture of virility and effeminacy.[27]

At the head of the group, a tall boy with sensuous lips and eyes with black rings under them carried a flag. It was Winnetou, the top man of the

---

26. For another colorful account of these events, see Heiden (491–94).

27. Howard Becker's descriptions of Roamers ca. 1900 suggest certain continuities to the 1930s. Their models were "wandering scholars of medieval times, robber knights . . . peasant Robin Hoods, defiant Gypsies, and savage chieftains" (75). Becker is contemptuous of testimony that suggests the early Roamers engaged in homosexual activity, accusing those who claimed this of "a strong note of self-justification." But he does speak, albeit disapprovingly, of one group, the Slicks, who at the war's end "seem merely to champion their own feminized variety of sexual inversion" (209).

gang. He wasn't very talkative, but he did say enough for us to grasp the essentials. We were dealing with a *Wild-clique*—a wild gang—a band of adolescents gone astray, asocials, a community of youths rejected by the larger community.

Upon returning to Berlin, I raced through the editorial offices of the far-left press to find someone who could fill me in about these "cliques." I was referred to Christine Fournier, the former wife of the liberal writer Rudolph Olden, and a collaborator on *AIZ* (*Arbeiter Illustrierte Zeitung*),[28] the illustrated weekly magazine published by Willy Munzenberg, the inspired speculator and Stalinist propagandist. Madame Olden had spent time with these young wastrels. With solicitude and patience she had succeeded in winning their confidence, getting herself admitted into their company, and penetrating their jealously guarded secrets. In the *Neue Weltbühne* of January 20, 1931, she recorded the fruits of her audacious observations in an excellent article.[29]

Before me stood a woman approximately forty-five years of age, with a face still young and attractive despite her prematurely gray hair. She had a sparkling gaze behind her tortoiseshell glasses. My vagabond's getup didn't seem to put her off too much; she was used to it.

"Where do these gangs come from?"

"In Germany, cliques are nothing new. They were born out of the chaos of the war and the postwar period. As early as 1916–1917, it was possible to run into troupes like this in the working-class districts [*faubourgs*] and suburbs of the large cities. They were made up of adolescents whose fathers were at the front and mothers in the factories. Nobody at home took care of them. The postwar inflation and the unemployment over the past two years have multiplied these gangs. For uprooted and often homeless youths, they offer a communal way of life, camaraderie, and a sense of danger and adventure. To escape the temptation of suicide, they create a fantasy world for themselves, a world that rests upon precepts that are completely different from those of accepted morality, a world given over to the most unbridled instinct, a world of hatred toward the society which has abandoned them."

28. *Workers' Illustrated Newspaper,* especially known for its anti-Nazi photomontage covers by John Heartfield. After the Nazis came to power, the paper was published for a time in Prague and smuggled into Germany.
29. It appears as the Appendix to this volume.

"Thus their motto, *Wild-frei?*"

"*Wild-frei,* wild and free, rebels against all authority. They are rebels, not revolutionaries. The names which the cliques give themselves are meaningful only to them: Blood of the Tartars, Blood of the Indians, Blood of the Cossacks, Wild Crime, Girls' Terror, Red Apaches, Black Love, Bloody Carcasses, Pirates of the Forest, and Schnapps Guzzlers. They've all read Karl May,* our Gustave Aimard,* and the surname Winnetou, which they're so fond of, belonged to the last of the Apaches."

"And their sex life?"

"Each clique has its shelter—in a barn, a cave, or a warehouse—and the only piece of furniture in this clandestine refuge is the *Stoszsofa,* the sofa where coitus occurs. But that's not all . . ."

My interlocutor lowered her voice: "There are secret rites of initiation . . . at night, in some deserted forest or on the shore of one of the many lakes that surround metropolitan Berlin. The trials are sometimes dreadful: knife fights, immersion fully clothed in the lake, trial by fire; the sex act performed by the initiate in front of the clique in a fixed amount of time determined by the chief, stopwatch in hand. But there's even worse . . ."

At that moment, Madame Olden, called to the telephone in a neighboring room, left me alone. I took advantage of the occasion to seize upon an envelope stuffed with photographs to which she had alluded but, of course, dared not show me. I fell upon a collection of naked adolescents hanging from branches by their wrists or tied up at the top of a tree with their hands behind their backs while members of the clique, also naked, brandished phallic emblems around them.

By the time Madame Olden returned, I had put the images back into the envelope.[30]

"The initiation celebration," she concluded, "always degenerates into a drunken binge, a mad orgy. What these youths have read, of course, may have played a certain role: perhaps they *are* imitating primitive rites. But I rather believe that it's really a matter of a spontaneous return to barbarism. Civilization, after all, is but a very thin, recent, and fragile veneer."

Taking my leave of Christine Fournier, I couldn't dismiss a real anxiety: those who would know how to discipline these masquerade Apaches could

---

30. Guérin gives an additional account of this episode in *Le feu du sang,* 29.

make real bandits out of them. Two years later, the journalist for the *Neue Weltbühne* (who had since become my mother-in-law) would confide to me that after Hitler came to power, she met a sinister and powerful SA member in a Berlin street. To her surprise, the Nazi called out to her in a familiar, even affectionate tone. Finally, she recognized him. It was the former chief of the clique whose friendship she had won. It was Winnetou.[31]

A world of distance separated Kuhle Wampe from the *Wild-clique*. Yet, both were products of the unemployment and poverty of the times. But in this instance, we're no longer dealing with rebels but with revolutionaries.

Kuhle Wampe, on the shores of the Muggelsee, was a camp for unemployed Berliners. In that summer of 1932, it had just served as the inspiration for a magnificent and exciting film by the Communist director Slatan Dudow* in collaboration with Bertolt Brecht,* and this brought an uninterrupted stream of visitors. Spread along the lakeshore, under the pines, the tiny dwellings all looked alike: simple wooden posts covered with white or zebra-striped tent canvas. All were well lit, clean, and well kept. The builders rivaled each other in ingenuity and whimsy. Miniature gardens surrounded the most beautiful constructions. At the moment of my arrival, an elderly unemployed couple stood in ecstasy, motionless, watering can in hand, before three still-dripping geraniums.

As it began to rain, a boy invited me to take shelter in his hut. He offered me a chair, the only one. Some residents took their places on stools made from rough wood, while others climbed onto bunk beds. I was surrounded by several solid comrades with frank expressions dressed in navy-blue overalls, and their young, smiling, attentive wives. They explained: "You see, the air at Kuhle Wampe is better than in our neighborhoods, and this is a vacation that doesn't cost a thing. We prefer to cycle to Berlin once a week to pick up our unemployment benefits. And we also want to show that proletarians know how to live an intelligent and liberated life."

When the rain stopped, we went down to the lakeshore to watch young and old alike give themselves over to the pleasures of sunbathing. The more cerebral were spread out on their blankets immersed in serious reading. As

---

31. Not all the *Wild-frei* wound up in the service of the Nazis. On the contrary, groups of youth continued to "wander" and hide in the forests throughout the years of Nazi rule, including the war years. Some of these groups actively harassed the Hitler Youth and engaged in other antigovernment activities; see Peukert (chap. 3).

I was getting ready to snap a picture, a tall, supple, and well-tanned athlete with a tawny mop of hair tore off his bathing suit with an abrupt gesture and offered himself entirely naked to the burning rays of the sun: "To protest against the ordinance of Chancellor von Papen!" he shouted, then burst out laughing.

In fact, the Reaction looked unfavorably upon these camps of free proletarians from which bourgeois prejudices had been banished. Several camps had already been outlawed, and a puritan ordinance prohibiting nudism had been declared. The unemployed of Kuhle Wampe were neither outlaws nor cranks, but healthy and resolute individuals who intended to make the best use of their period of forced idleness. For them, nature worship and nudism were not pretexts for exhibitionism nor a diversion from social struggles. They loved the sun that made them stronger, and the clothes they cast off in a challenge to the barons of the Herrenklub symbolized the prejudices they were rejecting.

The Communists of Wedding, the Red quarter of Berlin, were found in great numbers at Kuhle Wampe; through patient argument they held at bay the individualistic, petit-bourgeois mentality that is a more or less permanent threat to a colony of campers.

A lost island in the midst of a Germany torn asunder, Kuhle Wampe would soon be swept aside by the Hitlerite tidal wave. All that would remain of it would be the unperishable images preserved in film libraries.

To visit the militants and the "theoreticians" of various political tendencies whose addresses I had been given, I crossed the length and breadth of Gross-Berlin. The elevated S-Bahns had me striking bold diagonals across the giant metropolitan area and tracing enormous concentric circles around it. I attended the meeting of a section of the Social Democratic party: old, routinist, obtuse, passive militants; prattling grandmothers who reminded me of our church ushers or ladies of the Red Cross, stout and staid petit bourgeois.

But, at the back of the room, an impatient group of youths fidgeted as if trying to shake off the lid that was suffocating them. Their spokespersons finally managed to get themselves heard and delivered an indictment fanned by their anger. The young generation broke into unbridled applause while the sullen older ones remained silent. Division ran deep through the hall. Nevertheless, when it came time to take to task the ministers who on July 20 had allowed themselves to be dislodged from the Prussian government by Chancellor von Papen without offering the least gesture of resistance, all the speakers, including a deputy from the Landtag [state parliament, in contrast to the Reichstag, the national parliament] were in agreement. A Socialist never quite gets over losing a minister's portfolio or a parliamentary seat![32]

Another evening, I was the guest at a meeting of a group of Young Communists in Red Wedding. In the back room of a café, youths—boys and girls—were seated around a large table. I admired their seriousness, their level of culture, their militant ardor. A very young man, perhaps seventeen, with glasses and determined gestures, solemnly opened the session. With a volubility and a savoir-faire that left me flabbergasted, he tried to justify (undoubtedly to convince himself) the party line. I would have preferred him less glib, for bewitching as he was, his sectarianism, far from disheartening his audience, reassured and cast a spell on it. It seemed to me that all his comradely devotion and revolutionary faith were being completely wasted.

The exception was a youth whose blond hair was illuminated by moonbeams through an open window. Alone in his views, his crystal-clear voice murmured this heresy: "The misfortune of our times is that there is no one to guide us in the midst of this chaos. Ah, if only Lenin were still alive!"

To tell the truth, throughout my entire trip I was unable to find a single Communist who, once feeling confident about me after a few moments of conversation, claimed to be *really* in agreement with the party's tactics. The most orthodox repeated to themselves that "the line is correct," but they did so with the anxiety of a believer assailed by doubt. As for the most courageous, they barely hid their unease.

I entered the unemployment bureau of a working-class neighborhood.

32. See the Introduction for a further discussion of the "Prussian coup." Konrad Heiden is certainly correct in claiming that the lack of resistance in Prussia, by far the largest and most powerful *Land* of the Republic, to the antidemocratic measures of the central government demonstrated that serious resistance to further attacks would likely be weak throughout the country. So obvious is this failure to Heiden that he summarizes his discussion with the terse sentence, "Thus ended the short-lived Weimar Republic" (474).

Long queues of resigned and mute men traced arabesques through the huge, airy, clean room. At the exit, the out-of-work lingered for as long as possible on the sidewalk. What was the point of hurrying? Wasn't this what one might call "the last of the salons where one finds good conversation"? And conversation once engaged in turned quickly into sharp political discussion. It was no longer at the factory or at the workshop that the three political parties cast their nets, but here. Leaflets and small mimeographed newspapers were abundantly distributed. Sometimes, a bloody scuffle would erupt between Reds and Browns.

A circle of slim young workers with navy-blue caps and glowing eyes grew as we watched. I drew near. An altercation pitted two of them against each other. They were shouting loudly and seemed on the verge of coming to blows. At first, I thought it was a dispute between a Nazi and a Communist. Instead, they were two hostile brothers.

The Social Democrat's appearance was typical: a serious and tidy worker, middle-aged, a little chubby. The Communist was younger, more bohemian, more passionate, and thinner as well. Before an audience that was keeping score, they threw in each other's faces all the errors, past and present, of their respective parties. The majority of the spectators visibly sided with the Communist. But the Socialist wasn't easily taken down, and he obstinately defended his leaders. The two were separated with great difficulty.

In spite of the resistance of the ruling bureaucracies, however, a tendency toward unity had been born at the base. Many workers finally understood that a common struggle against the fascist peril was a matter of life or death. In July and August, following the Prussian coup d'état, a united front "at the top"—that is, between organizations—was spontaneously achieved in a great number of places. But each time, it had barely been sealed when it came apart. Elsewhere, negotiations entered into were almost as quickly broken off. The central leaderships of the two workers' parties—in spite of strong pressure from the base—remained irreducibly opposed to united action: the Social Democrats for fear of losing the leadership of their troops, the Communists through servile obedience to Moscow's orders and the fear of going back on their own word by negotiating with "social fascists."

Each time, the burning question of the "truce on criticism" was the pretext for refusing to form a united front, and in particular for rejecting the proposals for a common general strike made on two separate occasions by the Communist party to the Social Democrats. The Communists refused to halt their ideological attacks against the reformists, while the latter would accept the united front only in the form of a truce of God where no expression of differences would be allowed to get under their much too sensitive skin.

And yet, the Communist party ought to have learned the lessons of its unsuccessful strike of July 20. How, without preparation, would it be possible to make workers indoctrinated with the hatred of "social fascism" lay down their tools and protest the expulsion of the "social fascist" ministers? But even more serious was the now obvious fact that while the party's influence was quite strong among the unemployed, it was practically nil among organized workers. Clearly, without the participation of the reformist workers a general strike was impossible. Since the party boasted that it would easily be able to lead millions of organized workers, what was it waiting for?

It took the tragic dénouement at the beginning of 1933—Hitler's accession to power, the burning of the Reichstag, the outlawing of the Communist party—before Moscow would authorize its subordinates to "renounce their attacks against the Socialist organizations during the period of common action." But by this time it was too late. Everything had already been engulfed by the Brown plague.

As they waited for their rapidly approaching final defeat, the luckless workers of Germany were cast into extreme disarray and confusion. I noted such comments as the following:

"Why must I, a Social Democrat worker, consider my main enemy to be my Communist workmate?"

"Why must I, a Communist worker, often come to lethal blows with the Nazi worker who's in line beside me at the unemployment bureau?"

Nobody, to tell the truth, knew the *why* of anything any longer. And so we saw Nazi workers take part in strikes against the Papen decrees. And we also saw the uncommitted drift from one camp to another with disconcerting ease: Social Democrats becoming Nazis, Nazis becoming Communists, and vice-versa. Nazis and Communists found common ground in their hatred of Social Democracy and in the poisonous slogan for National

Liberation. Socialists and fascists found common ground in the myths of a centralized economy and apolitical trade unionism integrated into the state structure.[33]

And above all, weariness took its toll. There was no sign of economic recovery. Would one ever find work again? The political parties had promised so much. So many posters had been read, so many leaflets had been skimmed. There had been so many electoral campaigns, so many ballots cast in vain. It was always the same old story. Even worse today than yesterday. The last liberties were being done away with, the workers' newspapers prohibited. In public meetings, I saw with my own eyes insolent Schupos cut off speakers who displeased them.

And from the most disoriented workers I heard this monologue, the death knell of democratic Germany: "Ah, if only the leaders could work together! But this is a remote and unlikely possibility. So why shouldn't I listen to these new saviors who promise bread and jobs, to free me from the chains of the Treaty of Versailles, and who swear that they are a revolutionary socialist workers' party, too? Heil Hitler!"

Yet, in the autumn of 1932 it might have seemed to the casual observer that the fascist tide was standing still or even receding. The gentlemen of the Herrenklub, supported by President Hindenburg* and the army, appeared for a moment to be consolidating their power. In the November 6 elections, engineered by Papen to replace the deputies of the Reichstag he had dissolved, the National Socialists lost seats.[34] The imprudent Léon Blum* lost no time pontificating in *le Populaire,*[35] "Hitler is henceforth excluded

---

33. Theodor Leipart, the leader of the Social Democratic trade unions, reminded his functionaries that although "the ultimate aim of the trade unions is the realization of socialism, [they] were established to improve the situation of the working class in the framework of the present economic order." He voiced support for the Schleicher government's job creation measures that overrode existing collective agreements: "The one and only thing we need now is a productive policy, resolute action to improve the situation of the German workers" (in Heiden, 502–3).

34. The Nazis returned 196 deputies, representing an actual loss of 34 seats from the previous Reichstag.

35. The newspaper Blum founded after the Tours Congress of 1920. Thereafter, *l'Humanité,* on which he had previously collaborated, became the organ of the French Communist party

from power. He is even excluded, if I may say so, from the hope of power. Between Hitler and power an impassable barrier has been raised."[36]

Chancellor von Papen was succeeded by an astute officer who had been his adjunct the day before. General von Schleicher* understood that a simple resurrection of the old imperial Germany, even the restoration of the monarchy, couldn't survive. The army, if it wished to channel or neutralize or even evict Hitler, had to come up with something new. Thus the general envisioned establishing, with the help of both the trade unions and the left wing of National Socialism, a kind of German "Bonapartism" or latent fascism: Prussian state capitalism with Mussolinian corporatism. He pilfered the Nazi and Socialist programs alike for rhetoric that could serve his ends. He picked up not only ideas but men in both camps. He flirted with Gregor Strasser, the Führer's demagogic rival,[37] while he struck deals with the equivocal Theodor Leipart.* This secretary general of the German equivalent of the CGT*[38] was a worthy emulator of our own Jouhaux.* Von Schleicher talked about nationalizing the banks and some large industries. The state apparatus would absorb some of Hitler's well-intentioned followers, who were merely in a bit of a hurry to demonstrate the extent of their talents. At the same time, he would integrate the union and cooperative *bonzes,* thus miraculously allowing them to keep their gilded fiefdoms.

But the plot was too byzantine, and too tardy, to succeed. Schleicher succeeded only in raising a coalition of adversaries against him from all

(PCF), or Section française de l'Internationale communiste (SFIC). Blum's paper entertained broad debate on socialist strategy and on the character of fascism.

36. November 9, 1932. Neither foes on the left nor the right forgave Blum this notorious false prophecy. Robert Brasillach integrates it into his account of France's somnambulance when confronted by Hitler's successes and the rebirth of German militarism (93).

37. In October 1925 Strasser started the *National Socialist Correspondence,* "which became as it were the 'theoretical' organ of the 'left' National Socialists." With his brother Otto, he started a small press in Berlin, the Kampf–Verlag, whose publications carried a very radical tone, intended to make the reader believe that he was being spoken to by a "friend of the workers" or even a "class fighter." Considering him too close to Schleicher, Hitler relieved Strasser of his functions in late 1932 (*BT,* 26–27).

38. The ADGB,* or General German Trade Union Federation. At the time Guérin was writing, the French CGT was Socialist in its allegiance. After the failure of the general strike of 1920, the majority faction and the anarcho-syndicalists constituted a new union, the CGTU (CGT unifiée), which affiliated with the Red International of Trade Unions in 1923 (Communist International). Reunification took place in 1936, with both unions adhering to the program of the Popular Front.

parties. How could the lower echelons of the union movement be expected to allow Leipart to chain himself to the general's chariot? Above all, even with the army's support how could one expect this improvised eleventh-hour Bonapartism to successfully hold onto power in the face of an entire people impatient for radical change?

And then a footnote, to which Brecht seems to have given priority with disappointing myopia in his *Arturo Ui*,[39] came to graft itself onto this larger historical tableau. Trying to cover up a bribery scandal which threatened to implicate him, the aged President Hindenburg dismissed Chancellor von Schleicher, whom he felt to be insufficiently obliging.[40] On January 30, 1933, at the instigation of Papen and his barons, he installed Hitler in power. The irreparable had been accomplished.[41]

On February 28, 1933,[42] a young Communist comrade whom I knew in Red Wedding sent a final message to me in France: Hitler's government, he wrote, was preparing a major action against the party. After the elections that were scheduled for March 5, the CP (KPD*) would be outlawed and the mandates of its elected members nullified. Public opinion was already being prepared for this *coup de force*. The proletariat was too weak to fight back. My correspondent added a gloomy postscript to his letter: he had just learned about the fire at the Reichstag that had broken out the previous night. Special editions were already spreading the official version: the Communists were responsible for the fire. "*I would love to find the idiot who*

39. Brecht's 1941 play, *Der aufhaltsame Aufstieg des Arturo Ui* (The resistable rise of Arturo Ui).

40. The so-called Osthilfe (Eastern Aid) scandal. Konrad Heiden refers to the "legend that Schleicher threatened Hindenburg with disclosure of the Eastern Aid scandal, and that Hindenburg hastily dropped his general and called Hitler to power, in the hope that Hitler should hush up the scandal (after his deputies had just voted for its exposure!). The truth is . . . that Schleicher demanded dictatorial powers [and Hindenburg] felt the weight of Schleicher's domination and shook it off when it became just a fraction of an ounce too much" (533–34).

41. Klaus Mann, who shares the cover-up interpretation of the Osthilfe scandal, captures the arrogance and overconfidence of those in the German establishment who opened the way to Hitler's accession to power: "The camarilla sold Germany, not for a potage of lentils, but for a piece of land and the vows of Mr. Adolf Hitler. . . . 'What is your Excellency waiting for?' urged Herr von Papen. 'It's just a formality. This man Hitler is our obedient tool. We, the friends of your Excellency and the pillars of order, will actually rule the country' " (1942: 258–59).

42. The original text says 1934, which is clearly a typographical error.

thought that by burning down the Reichstag he was acting in the interests of the German proletariat!" exclaimed my young correspondent. He continued: the National Socialist government, losing no time, had just decided to take severe measures against the party. Arrests and countless searches had already been carried out; the Nazi auxiliary police had been called to arms; a state of siege would be proclaimed; Berlin resembled a fortified camp; mass executions were not far off.[43] An unspeakable terror was about to be unleashed against the working class; and as the privacy of the mail would undoubtedly be violated, my correspondent ended his final message with these words: *"This letter will probably be the last."*[44] Night had fallen on Germany.

43. The Reichstag fire and its aftermath are discussed at length in the Introduction. In 1933 alone, the Reichstag fire decree was used as the basis for 3,584 criminal proceedings resulting in 3,133 sentences (*ETR*, 1991, 2:786–87).

44. After listing the articles of the Constitution that are suspended, the decree continues: "Consequently restrictions on personal freedom and on the right of free expression of opinion, including the freedom of the Press, and of the right of association and assembly, are permissible beyond the limit laid down in these articles of the Constitution. In addition, the privacy of correspondence, of the post, telegraph and telephonic service is suspended, and house-searchings and the confiscation or restriction on the rights of property are permissible" (*BT,* 70–71).

AFTER THE CATASTROPHE

1 9 3 3

Translator's Note: This section appears as "Après la catastrophe (1933)" in La Peste brune *(Paris: François Maspero, 1978, © 1963). Modifications from an earlier version,* La Peste brune a passé par là *(Paris: Editions Universelles, 1945) are indicated in two ways: Major divergences between the two versions are set off clearly in the main body of the text; minor changes are recorded in the footnotes.*

n April and May 1933, with Hitler now in power, I set out on another trip to Germany. This time, I went by bicycle, not on foot. Before leaving, I went to see Léon Blum and told him about my plans. Without hesitation, he gave me carte blanche. If he had been mistaken in certain overly optimistic prognoses in the fall of 1932, he had by now grasped the enormity of the disaster. My reports would appear a few weeks later in the SFIO's daily newspaper, *le Populaire*.[1]

I would like to add two picturesque details that I dared not mention in 1933. While on the road, this cyclist acquired the habit of hiding, in the tube of his bicycle frame, illegal tracts confided to him by clandestine militants. One day, on a bicycle path in Berlin, I collided with a woman; the shock broke the frame. Seeing the black leather cap of a policeman on the horizon, I fled on foot, carrying my compromising vehicle on my shoulder.

At the private Nazi meeting which I succeeded in attending in Leipzig, I gave the Roman salute along with everyone else and, blushing, shouted "Heil Hitler!" whenever called for. By engaging in this disgusting mimicry, I made sure I wasn't noticed and was able to accomplish my task as a reporter.

Back in France, I was stupefied to discover that my eyewitness account was met with incredulity, even within the Socialist party. The late Oreste Rosenfeld, then editor in chief of *le Populaire*, has since admitted to me that he received many letters of protest from readers, some of which were quite vehement. Surely I was exaggerating! Surely my mind had already been made up! The French Left still had a lot to learn.

1. The articles appeared from June 25 to July 13, 1933.

PREFACE TO THE
1945 EDITION

Today, alas, the French no longer need to be told about Nazi barbarism. The Brown tide that swept over Germany in 1933 has since passed over our own soil. It has only just receded. We have not yet healed from its wounds.

This account, however, will not provide the reader with yet another occasion for condemnation. For this, there is already ample cause. The images that I will parade before you will perhaps induce other reflections. For four years, all we saw of Germany was the bestial face of Hitlerism. It is not at all surprising, then, that we have come to confuse these brutes with the German people. This "documentary" reminds us that there is another Germany. It bears proof that the best of the German working class, far from being Hitler's accomplice, was the first victim of Brown barbarism.

It reminds us that this other Germany, after vainly attempting to stem the Hitlerite tide, continued a heroic underground struggle in the camps and prisons, during a terror parallel to that under which we waged our clandestine resistance.

The French worker Timbaud recognized this when he shouted "Long live the German Communist party!" before his firing squad.

Those deported to the Buchenwald camp were also of the same opinion. Immediately following their liberation, they wrote in a mimeographed edition of *l'Humanité:*[1] "We know that there are two Germanys—one that is Hitler's that must be exterminated, the other an antifascist Germany that must be helped." The French Communists in captivity, aided and some-

1. The newspaper of the French Communist party.

times even saved from death by their German Communist companions, were able to attest under hardship to the meaning of international proletarian solidarity. They refused to confuse the two Germanys, to equate Nazis and anti-Nazis, executioners and victims.

Even in France under the Occupation, despite the iron discipline of Prussian militarism and the terror of the ss,* Wehrmacht soldiers answered appeals written to them in their own language by clandestine groups of French workers and German refugees. For having read or distributed these tracts, French and German, civilian and soldier, were united by the same savage repression.

Despite all the instructions for "nonfraternization" issued on both sides by the belligerent states, workers stretched out their hands and succeeded in reaching each other.

The International today is but a tiny flame against the worldwide onslaught of barbarism. But it still burns, and that is already something, enough so that humankind does not despair of its future.

I dedicate these few pages to the memory of the German workers who gave their lives in the struggle against fascism; in particular, to that of my friend Arno Barr from Leipzig, a Communist militant. Arno helped me edit *La Peste brune*. He fell before Madrid at the end of 1936. "Madrid will be the tomb of fascism," he had written me a few days before. He was in error only about the date and the place.

The appalling regime which did such violence to the German people and then to Europe is now nothing more than an awful memory. But the struggle is not over; oppression of man by man has not ceased. In Germany itself, the workers have left one form of servitude only to fall into another. Elsewhere (in Greece and in the colonial nations), "liberating" planes and tanks are used to keep people in bondage.

And so the veil is torn away and we see a little more clearly. Already, we perceive, and every day we understand a bit better, that the real war doesn't take place between nations or peoples but between classes.

Tomorrow, national hatreds that were yesterday exacerbated beyond all measure will give way to the international solidarity of the exploited, to the people's common hatred of the exploiters. The anachronistic "To each his

Boche" will be superseded in all countries by the battle cry of our century: "To each his capitalism."

Together with the German workers, we will make the United Soviet Socialist States of Europe.

Rest in peace, Arno.

1   *The Tidal Wave*

few hundred kilometers from here, men like us move about in a different world, a closed world, where none of the things that comprise our habits of thought, feeling, or struggle are any longer permitted. Last year, having a foreboding of the catastrophe, I wanted to get to know the Socialist and revolutionary Germany that has today been trampled, assassinated.

When I close my eyes, I see once more those great crowds of ardent and disciplined workers, those beautiful—too beautiful—People's Houses; I hear the virile singing of proletarian youth. I reflect upon that slow but certain movement toward unity in action which, at the very deepest levels, was winning over the masses . . .

The Brown plague passed there.

What exactly are its ravages? What remains of the Germany that we knew, understood, and loved?

I have returned there. On bicycle, from Cologne to Hamburg, from Hamburg to Berlin and to Leipzig, mixing with men in the cities and the countryside, lodging, as last year, in those youth hostels that are themselves a microcosm of the Germanic spirit, I have tried to see, to hear, to explain.

A socialist traveling beyond the Rhine today has the impression of exploring a city in ruins after an earthquake. Here, only a few months ago, was the headquarters of a political party, a trade union, a newspaper; over there was a workers' bookstore. Today, enormous swastika banners hang from these buildings. This used to be a Red street; they knew how to fight here. Today, one meets only silent men, their gazes sad and worried, while the children shatter your eardrums with their "Heil Hitler!"s.

All that we loved in Germany yesterday, everything that we will see again some day in the Germany of tomorrow, has been overrun, though not annihilated, by the Brown tide. One has to go deep into people's homes and hearts to find the class consciousness, the warm camaraderie, the sense of collective life, the maturity and cultivation, the revolutionary faith that have been and still are the virtues of our German comrades. Despite all the determined efforts to extinguish it, that flame still burns, but in the shadows and in silence. On the other hand, the other Germany struts about in broad daylight with all its meanness, its evil instincts awakened, its brutality, and the stomping of its boots. How can I tell you what one feels in such a country? It is impossible, I believe, to love more and hate more at the same time.

Yet, you have to overcome your repulsion and try to understand. It is easy enough to pronounce anathema over these "Brown bandits," but the Hitlerite wave is such an extraordinary phenomenon (in the proper sense of the term) that vengeful epithets aren't enough to explain it. It surged forth from the depths of the German people. It's because of its popular appeal that it was irresistible, that it swept everything else away; that the workers' parties, divided among themselves, couldn't form a front against it; that the old reactionary and feudal Germany had to reluctantly make way for it.

Certainly, the dregs of the population have found asylum in the Brown army. There, they wield truncheons and play with guns to their hearts' content. But behind them are the peasant masses suffering from their low wages; the entire middle class in decomposition, those petit bourgeois ruined by inflation, by the crisis, struggling against the competition posed by big capital, against the proletarianization that faces them; and there are also broad working-class layers whose nerves have been wrecked by hunger and idleness; and most of all youth, without bread, work, or future.

You have to have seen with your own eyes how Germany has suffered these past years—and suffers more each day—not, of course, to excuse it, but to understand. You have to have known the queues at the unemployment bureau—the essential act in a life without acts—the piece of bread that takes the place of a meal, the unemployed youths who, with empty bellies, wander the roads of Germany or sing their plaint in the courtyards of working-class dwellings, to discover the secret of this collective, pathological, desperate madness.

Daniel Guérin, ca. 1928, and in the
Reichstag, September 1932. Courtesy
of Daniel Guérin.

Two of Daniel Guérin's eyewitness accounts of life in the final months of the Weimar Republic appeared in the French illustrated magazine *Vu*. These served as the basis for "Before the Catastrophe," the 1932 section of *La peste brune*. Reprinted from *La haine brune*.

Food Service Workers hiking club. Hiking was a popular pastime engaged in by political organizations, trade unions, religious associations, and youth groups. Photo by Daniel Guérin, courtesy of Fondation Mémoire des Sexualités, Paris.

Left: Christine Fournier published her article on the "Ring" gangs in *Die neue Weltbühne*. The journal was denounced by the Nazis as a "scandal-sheet." By 1938, it was being published in exile and smuggled into Germany. Reprinted from *Neues Volk* 6 (1938).

Four "Roamers" in 1932. Unlike those who participated in the structured hiking clubs, "wandering" was the fate of many unemployed German youths. Courtesy of Daniel Guérin.

Winnetou, the "chief" befriended by Christine Fournier. He took his name from the Indian chief in a novel by Karl May. On his belt are the words *Wild-frei* (wild and free).

A demonstration in Berlin on the anniversary of the Treaty of Versailles. The banner reads "Day of Versailles, Day of Disgrace!"; one placard proclaims, "We want to be free of Versailles!" Nazi propaganda played upon popular resentment at the heavy burden of reparations exacted by the treaty and its unfavorable boundary determinations. German government officials who signed the treaty were branded "traitors" and the "November criminals." Reprinted from *Das Jahr* I (a yearbook of the Nazi regime).

"Hitlerite Sundays." This photo appeared in the Nazi magazine *Neues Volk* with the caption "In the time of the System [i.e., the Weimar Republic], Negro bands played at dances. . . . Today we hear the sounds of joyous folk dances in the open air on national holidays." Reprinted from *Neues Volk* 6 (1938).

Hitler's first cabinet: "The Reich Cabinet of national salvation of January 30, 1933." Commemorative photo published in *Das Jahr* 1, the yearbook of the Nazi regime. *Seated left to right:* Göring, Hitler, von Papen; *standing left to right:* Seldte, Graf Schwerin-Krosigk, Dr. Frick, General von Blomberg, Dr. Hugenberg.

Mordhetze gegen jüdische Wissenschaftler

Juden
sehen
Dich
an

Wiedergabe des Buchumschlags
und von Unterschriften aus dem
Buch ‹Juden sehen Dich an.›
Diese von dem Naziabgeordne-
ten von Leers geschriebene
Broschüre hetzt offen zum Mord.
Der Beschreibung und dem Foto
zahlreicher deutscher Männer
des deutschen Geisteslebens ist
das Wort ‹Ungehängt› hinzu
gefügt.
Albert Einstein, der be-
rühmte Wissenschaftler erhob
unerschrocken seine Stimme
gegen den Hitlerterror.

Bildunterschriften. Abschnitt II: Lügenjuden

Einstein
Erfand eine stark bestrittene „Relativitätstheorie". Wurde von der Juden-
presse und dem ahnungslosen deutschen Volke hoch gefeiert, dankte dies
durch verlogene Greuelhetze gegen Adolf Hitler im Auslande. (Ungehängt.)

"Jews Are Watching You": the cover of the infamous book as reproduced in the German edition of *The Brown Book of the Hitler Terror.* Also included is the entry on Albert Einstein, whose theory of relativity is mocked. Einstein is accused of spreading "atrocity propaganda" abroad, and the entry concludes "not [yet] hanged." Reprinted from *Braunbuch über Reichtagsbrand und Hitler-Terror.*

A page from the Nazi magazine *Neues Volk* vilifying Dr. Magnus Hirschfeld, the great Berlin sex researcher and reformer. Hirschfeld, a Jew, a Social Democrat, and a homosexual, escaped the Nazis but his institute was sacked and the library burned. The article, entitled "The Wandering Jew," also denounces religious Jews ("Talmuden-juden") and the Russian revolutionary leader Leon Trotsky. Reprinted from *Neues Volk* 6 (January 1938).

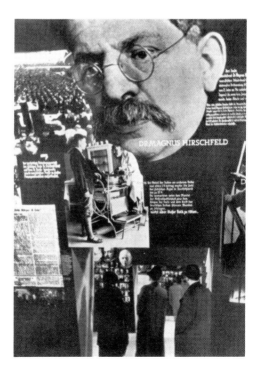

This depiction of a German school lesson appeared in *Neues Volk* in 1934. The chart is No. 1 in the series "Races of the Earth: Europe and Its Periphery." The teacher instructs his students on the "ideal Nordic type of youth," with a fine example standing in the foreground. Reprinted from *Neues Volk* 2 (July 1934).

The Eldorado Club boarded up and covered with Nazi posters. The Eldorado was a popular gay bar in Berlin, which fell victim to a series of "anti-smut" raids shortly after the Nazi seizure of power. The club's windows have been covered with Nazi posters in preparation for the March 5, 1933, Reichstag elections. Police guard the posters against "vandalism." Reprinted by permission of Landesbildstelle Berlin.

Poupées d'enfants au troisième Reich. «Et nous commençons l'entraînement chez l'enfant dès l'âge de trois ans . . . »
Puppen für Kinder im dritten Reich. «Und so fangen wir schon beim Kinde von drei Jahren an . . »
Dolls for children in the third Reich. «And so we commence already with the child at three years of age . . . »
Dr. Robert Ley.
«Nationalsozialistische Monatshefte»

Above Left: "All of Brown Berlin shops at Kohnen! Brown uniforms, business suits, gentlemen's apparel. . . ." This advertisement appeared in the Nazi party handbook, *Führer durch den Nationalsozialismus* (Forward to National Socialism). It is typical of ads that appeared in a range of Nazi journals and magazines.

Above Right: "It's dangerous at night! A flashlight that no SA or SS man should be without! Produced only with German materials, labor, and capital. . . ." Another ad from the Nazi handbook *Führer durch den Nationalsozialismus.*

Left: Dolls for children in the Third Reich. "And so we commence already with the child at three years of age. . ." (Dr. Robert Ley). Reprinted from *La haine brune.*

A contingent from Wedding, the famous "Red" working-class district of Berlin, on the "National Day of Labor," May 1, 1933. This photo appeared in the Nazi yearbook *Das Jahr* with a caption extolling the "unity" that had been achieved within the German proletariat, now marching under the common banner of the swastika. On the following day the trade unions were "coordinated" into the German Labor Front. Reprinted from *Das Jahr* 1.

Father and sons. This photo appeared in the Nazi magazine *Neues Volk* with the caption "Im Ehrenkleid der Bewegung" (in the honorable uniform of the Movement). Reprinted from *Neues Volk* 6 (1938).

Clandestine publications, artisanally produced. Titles include *Workers' World* and *Truth*. Reprinted from *Braunbuch über Reichstagsbrand und Hitler-Terror*.

"Willy, a young German Communist refugee in France. Together, we went camping—chastely. I never dared go any further, despite his superb body" (Daniel Guérin). Photo by Daniel Guérin, courtesy of Fondation Mémoire des sexualités, Paris.

Willy with his French peasant hosts. Photo by Daniel Guérin, courtesy of Fondation Mémoire des sexualités, Paris.

Daniel Guérin, ca. 1977. Photo by Sophie Bassouls,
courtesy of Daniel Guérin.

In a confused and diverse way, this immense mass cries for a *socialism* to which it considers itself predestined and that it expects will put an end to its suffering. They are convinced that Hitler will now give them this socialism, which the workers' parties had promised for the previous fourteen years but never succeeded in delivering. Peasants in the east who hope for land redistribution, small shopkeepers who demand protection against big capital, proletarians whom only a "revolution" can satisfy; these are the men and women who form the tidal wave which nothing has been able to resist, which blindly continues its surge forward.

How far will it go? It's true that the trajectory of this meteor cannot be calculated in advance. But what is certain is that it is still advancing at a constant speed. One day, it will have to culminate in some terrible accident or shock . . .

Thrust forward by this current, the supreme leaders hasten with unheard-of speed and malevolent fever to build for eternity in the space of a few weeks. In all the cities and towns, the main squares have been given the name of Adolf Hitler. Not to mention the Goebbels schools or the Hermann Göring foundations. Their speeches obsessively repeat that the Third Reich will last until the end of time. Decree follows upon decree, appointment upon appointment, law upon law.

Needless to say, one searches in vain for the slightest trace of *socialism* in these improvisations. But one already finds a surprising sense of organization (we *are* in Germany), an incontestable audacity, and at the same time a puerile and vulgar cynicism.

Of course, under the pressure of the masses—and to maintain control as long as possible—the possessing classes will be constrained to make a few sacrifices.

But eight million unemployed and their families wait for bread; and the thirst for socialism lies deep in the German heart.

In anticipation of the day, which is not so far off, when the masses realize that they have been duped, the Nazi leaders believe they have time to cement their power so strongly, and establish such a colossal secret police,[1] that they will be able to resist any storm.

First, we shall visit the adversary, the victors of the hour. Then, we shall

---

1. The 1945 edition has "Cheka" instead of "secret police," the former being the original name of the Soviet secret police. The Gestapo was created on April 26, 1933.

search out our friends of the *other Germany*—small groups of staunch militants who have put the fratricidal quarrels of the past behind them and who continue the struggle under conditions of illegality and terror. They will greet us with this simple sentence: "We have remained true to what we were."

The Brown plague passed here, but they were not cut down.

2 *Youth Gone Mad*

To begin, you must follow me among madmen. If you have trouble understanding, that's regrettable. But you will do as I have done and master your nerves.

As I look back and seek the precise date of my entry into this fantastic realm, one image stands out: the youth hostel in Essen one Sunday afternoon. Essen, the grim, sad, gray working-class city, Krupp's city . . . Last year in this shelter, you would have found tranquil lodgers[2] busy preparing their evening meal.

But today, the common room is full to the bursting point, not with young vagabonds but with the sons and daughters of the Essen proletariat. How hot it is! A musty smell, the smell of leather. For the majority of these young workers are decked out in boots and belts; and the tie of the Hitler Youth lies across their khaki shirts like a black stain. The girls are wearing tiny brown vests that are very masculine, very military with the swastika insignia in the buttonhole.

Never before had I felt so uneasy in a youth hostel. I felt out of place. Would I be asked to leave? No, they behaved as if I wasn't there. They treated me with a haughty disdain; they didn't even make the effort to find out what a foreigner—a man from the other world, a man who didn't click

2. In the 1945 edition, Guérin retains the German *Wanderers* instead of the more neutral *usagers* in the later edition. He adds in a footnote: "This word is untranslatable; 'vagabond' perhaps comes closest, except in French it has a pejorative connotation. By using the German term, I mean those young people who travel on foot with a backpack. Today, we'd call them 'ajistes'" [the French term deriving from *auberge de jeunesse,* or "youth hostel"—trans.].

■ *89*

his heels, a man who says "Bonjour!" and not "Heil Hitler!"—might have felt.

There are musicians, guitarists, in this conglomeration of young people, among this adolescent soldiery. I thought about those charming road songs, so tender and bohemian, that I'd heard the previous year. But the time is long past for romanticism. They pluck the strings of their instruments with iron fingers and bellow forth, like one man, the hymns of the day: "The Storm Troopers are on the march . . . Hitler's flag calls us to battle . . ." Not a moment of respite. It would have been nice to hear a joke, a gallant word, a sonorous laugh. Without catching their breath, they begin again. They go through the entire repertory; the windows shake.

Undoubtedly, when you sing in chorus you don't feel hunger; you aren't tempted to seek out the *how* and *why* of things. You must be right, since there are fifty of you, side by side, crying out the same refrain.

They go through everything, even the "patriotic" melodies of old Germany. The enemy, the *Franzose*, takes it on the chin, just like the *Boche* in our jingoistic songs.

A youth next to me, less fanatical than the others, leans over and whispers in my ear: "I hope you don't understand the words."

But the others are incapable of feeling the same concern.

Finally, there is a lull. Just to say something, I allude to the poverty, to the eight million unemployed.

"Not *now!*" interrupts one of the boys, about twelve years old, in a tone of surprise and reproach.

And the others, in chorus, are more explicit: "Hitler has promised that in four years there will be no more unemployment."

I would hear this mechanical, inevitable reply day after day, week after week, from the mouths of adolescents, adults, and the elderly.

The hostel warden, a Krupp worker in a proletarian blue cap, contemplates this amazing spectacle from the doorway. But he bows his head and remains silent.

I respect his silence. So many efforts and so much struggle in the proletarian Ruhr Valley, only for it all to come to this!

In Lübeck, it's even worse. The youth hostel, which only yesterday was the home of the Young Socialists, is now occupied by the Brownshirts. The hostel warden is a young SA sporting boots and straps. He is very courteous. Whenever one asks him for information, he comes to attention, clicks his heels, and gives the concise reply of a well-drilled orderly.

Some Storm Trooper sections have been staying in the hostel for a few days, and the musty barracks aroma still wafts vaguely through the air. From morning till evening, the Hitler Youth of the city choose the large shaded courtyard—where it would have been so nice to lie daydreaming— for lining up in ranks and performing their impeccable "Right, right's" and "Left, left's." "Fall-in," "fall-out"; uniform inspections; nothing is omitted.

During a rest period, a young warrior comes to sit beside me and strikes up a conversation in a comradely tone: "In France, do you have National Socialists in uniform, too?"

My negative reply seems to disappoint him. He had been told so many times that fascism is spreading like an oil stain . . .

And when I chance a few criticisms, he leans on the table with his elbows and states with deep conviction: "Look, haven't we saved the planet from Bolshevism?"

My impression is that this is an absolutely closed world with which no contact is possible. What's the use of talking? What we have to say would no longer be understood. These crazed primitives work each other up, cut off from the rest of the world.

———

"We learned by telephone this morning that thirty-eight French spies are in the region," one of the young SA's announces to me in a tone that is both serious and cordial.

I'm from a country where people still have the maddening habit of wanting to discuss things: "How could thirty-eight spies be all together? Normally, spies work alone."

"That's what we mean. Each is alone, but altogether, there are thirty-eight," affirm my young SA's with stubborn conviction.

And since I decide it is useless to reply, one of them looks me straight in the eye: "Do you know what's done to spies in all countries?"

"Are you saying this for my benefit?"

"No, but do you know what they do?"

"Tell me, what?"

"They hang them!"

And with his hand, he traces a rope around his neck.

In an attempt to dissipate the sinister thoughts of these youths, I offer them cigarettes.

Barely have I the time to smoke one when an ss man, wearing his black cap decorated with the death's-head, advances toward me with a quick step. He halts about three meters from me:

"The police want to see your papers. Would you follow me?"

"Yes, of course."

Alas! my papers were in order and I wasn't one of the thirty-eight.

As I am about to leave the next morning, the hostel warden, relieved, amicable, and clicking his heels, announces to me: "Good news! We just got a call from Rostock: The thirty-eight French spies have been arrested. Until we have the pleasure of meeting again . . . Heil Hitler!"

3 *Hitlerite Sundays*

O n the seventh day of each week, the collective madness knows no bounds.

It begins at seven in the morning with the loudspeakers: the "Horst Wessel Song," national revolution, Germany awake. . . . You spring out of bed, your nerves already on edge. On the wall, a giant portrait of Adolf completes the intoxication. The red flags with the swastikas are taken out; they're so large that the downstairs neighbors have to forgo sunlight. The cup of ersatz coffee is quickly downed; what does it matter if the humble slice of black bread doesn't fill the stomach? Germany has awakened; life is beautiful.

In the *Beobachter,* you read the program of the day. From eight o'clock to nine, there's a concert by the Forty-second Storm Trooper section on the Adolf Hitlerplatz. Delegations of veterans have come in from the countryside in their old uniforms, wearing the pointed helmets and pea jackets of the death hussars.

"Hurry, Otto! Tighten your belt. Let's not miss a minute of this beautiful show!"

Otto's little sisters go wild when they begin to hear the first sounds of boots resonating on the pavement.

"Oh, Mama, it's the SA . . ."

On the lips of these crazed girls the prestigious sounds "SA," "SS" sound like the buzz of insects before a nocturnal storm. Without boots, without the aroma of leather, without the rigid and severe stride of a warrior, it's impossible today to conquer these Brunhildes. In Hitlerism, there are deeply disturbing sexual components.

The orchestra has finished playing. Everyone remains at attention, gives the Roman salute, and the conductor responds in the same way to the applause. For the thousandth time, the electrifying verses are taken up in chorus. And now, in every neighborhood, in front of the beer hall that serves as the headquarters for their respective organizations, the SA, the SS, and the Hitler Youth assemble. Obese mothers moved to tears watch the spectacle from the windows of the surrounding houses. The young boys are already in line, immobile, their heads high, their chins tightened under their headgear. Roll call, inspection. "At ease!"

A young leader with a raw voice hurls out the resounding words: "You are the unknown soldiers of the Brown army. Always be ready to die for Hitler, for the revolution, for the Fatherland!"

This youth section has organized a hike in the countryside. Two vans decorated with greenery and flags are parked alongside the sidewalk. But before thinking about the joys of nature, there's a little propaganda to be done. The neighborhood, only yesterday still very Marxist, is far from won over. And so, they set out at a quick pace, hammering the streets, and with already virile voices these adolescents begin to sing out a marching song stolen from the Communists in which the words "left . . . left" return over and over again like a leitmotiv.[3] Were it not for the brown uniforms, one could believe that these were the proud Red Front fighters, the former masters of the streets. In the windows and despite the swastikas, the flags, like yesterday, are the color of blood.

The demonstration over, the youths crowd into the vehicles. Until evening, amidst an odor of sweat and leather, they will untiringly bawl out their songs and drunkenly give the Roman salute.

At eleven o'clock, announces the *Beobachter,* there will be a large assembly of SA and SS on the esplanade. Sections converge from all over. The commands crisscross, heels click, the crowd gets larger by the minute. Lots of petit bourgeois, lots of women, few proletarians.

An elderly man, well dressed—a retired professor, formerly a person of independent means ruined by inflation?—exhales his love of the Führer in

3. The song is "Roter Wedding" (Red wedding), named after the militantly Communist working-class neighborhood of Berlin. It was composed by Hans Eisler.

his neighbor's ear: "That man is ready to give his last drop of blood for us . . ."

Soon, the esplanade is but a vast human square with brown and black caps. The men have been on their feet for an hour now.

Finally, the big chiefs arrive, ridiculously strapped up, their fat asses compressed into their tight shorts. Reviewing the troops. Thousands of men at attention. Then, the inevitable speech broadcast over the loudspeakers exalting the national revolution. Hollow words, crass and primitive eloquence, but expertly calculated. The speaker, a *von* someone or other, undoubtedly a former officer of Wilhelm II, knows how to forget his refined language for the occasion. And his hoarse vociferations stir these embittered and half-starved unemployed youths to their entrails.

Rain has begun to fall. Soon, it's pouring. The brown shirts, now soaked, take on an earthy color. No one flinches. The speech goes on for yet another hour under sheets of water. Only, from time to time, a space opens up in the ranks. A man falls from cold and hunger. Discreet nurse-orderlies quickly evacuate him.

"Heil! Heil! Heil!" five thousand icy breasts finally shout by way of conclusion.

Then, one after the other, the sections move off. The Sunday training march has begun. Thirty kilometers through the countryside, music leading the way.

Before each flag, chubby petit bourgeois give the Roman salute. I watch the monotonous parade, the gaggle of skinny youths. Here and there among them, a conspicuous adult mustache or gray hair. These are the cadres, the NCOs of the imperial army, the men who can be depended upon . . .

Workers in civilian dress, insignia on their lapels, join the line: ordinary party members, they too won over by the demonic attraction of the march, or members of the National Socialist Works Cells Organization (NSBO).* As if to seek pardon for their nonmilitary garb, they sing more loudly than the others.

In a deafening sputtering of engines, the motorcycle brigades move to the fore: two men per machine, following one after the other at regular intervals and at a wild speed. They look like they're setting out on some punitive expedition.

Marschieren . . . marschieren, the magical word on which all of Germany becomes intoxicated today, is repeated in every verse of every hymn, every time a speech is given, in the tirades of every pen pusher. Everyone's on the march. Everyone will march straight ahead until evening falls.

Without catching their breath, they will pass through villages that are all decked out and stricken by the fever: three-year-old children will stiffen and shout their "Heil Hitler!" Other troops on the march will be encountered, for every village is on the march.

———————

Everywhere—from the city to the smallest hamlet—these heady Sundays are the same. It's Hitler in person, or Goebbels, or Göring who descends from the heavens with the roar of an airplane to take the temperature of the masses and push them toward a paroxysm. Everything is a pretext for rejoicing: the anniversary of a battle, of a national hero, or of the triumphs of an ancient regiment.

Every Sunday the bunting is taken out and everyone marches; and every Sunday, it begins all over again.

When night falls, they still want more, and so whether in the humble barn or the great festival hall, a "German evening" is held with music and speeches. Then, there's the torchlight recessional.

Eleven o'clock. There's nothing left on the program announced in the *Beobachter.* Look at this dignified petit-bourgeois couple returning home. The swastika glows ostentatiously on their breasts. No doubt their fever's still ablaze!

But doubt *is* already at work on their subconscious. The man whispers into the ear of his wife, "All these festivities are very nice, but they don't put bread on the table."

4 *Their Propaganda*

Brothers, reach for the sun, for freedom!" sang the Socialists and the Communists to an old and stirring popular melody:[4]

> Break the yoke of the tyrants
> Who so cruelly oppress you,
> And brandish the blood red flag
> Above the workers' world!

With total disingenuousness, the Nazis have appropriated this song, just as they have done with the red flag, May Day, dramatic recitations, the five-year plans, and a thousand other things. The *blood red* flag has simply become the *swastika* flag, and the workers' *world,* considered too internationalist, has become the workers' *state.*

No need to exercise your brain. What's essential is that the masses maintain the illusion of singing a revolutionary song.

But this is only pilfering. Faithfully imitating Italian fascism, the Nazis have stolen something much more important from communism, a prestigious word and art: *Propaganda.*

The most astute of the leaders of National Socialism, the tiny Dr. Goebbels, isn't afraid to devote a ministry to it. It's a scientific, modern advertising organization that has given Hitler's party its formidable power of expansion. The Brown bandits will eventually become men of state, but they've already been prodigious film directors for some time! You should

4. The German title of the song is "Brüder, zur Sonne, zur Freiheit." The song was originally composed by the Russian scientist Leonid P. Radin in 1879 while in a tsarist prison in Moscow. The German lyrics are by Hermann Scherchen. It was often sung in workers' parades to a march tempo.

hear Goebbels swoon in admiration over *The Battleship Potemkin,* while of course prohibiting the showing of Eisenstein's film in the Third Reich.

The Soviet state publishers have certainly never produced such an avalanche of books within such a short period. A week after May Day, the display windows of the bookstores were already packed with handsomely laid-out and moderately priced albums illustrating the National Day of Labor. Countless works foster the cult of the Führer: *How Adolf Hitler Became the Leader, Hitler Rules, Hitler's Native Land, The Hitler Nobody Knows, Hitler and His Warriors, Triumph of the Will.* Innumerable monographs on Goebbels, Göring, and Frick* are hastily and poorly edited, then put on sale. One of Goebbels's panegyrists is none other than a bureau chief at the Ministry of Propaganda: one is never better served than by one's own.

Alongside these garish productions are the "classics." In the forefront, the two volumes of *Mein Kampf.* Hundreds of thousands of copies of Hitler's autobiography, written in prison in 1925 following the failed Munich putsch, have been sold and are being sold every day. Goebbels's *Fight for Berlin,* Rosenberg's *Myth of the Twentieth Century,* Feder's *Struggle Against High Finance* and *The German State,* and Moeller van den Bruck's *Germany's Third Empire* are the indispensable, "fundamental" works.[5] And for the masses, there are innumerable popularized brochures: *The Party Program, The ABCs of National Socialism, How I Became a National Socialist,* etc. . . .

Naturally, you'll find all the heroes of the day on postcards, and if you desire a portrait of the Führer there is a surfeit of choices. They come in black-and-white, in color, in all sizes, under glass or framed in gold. For over an hour now, a robust and corpulent blonde woman has been lovingly caressing the frames presented to her without being able to choose.

People who time and time again have contemplated this banal, expressionless face, the dark wisp of hair, the bit of mustache, the well-waxed shoulder strap, still stop in front of the shop windows and defenselessly surrender to the hypnotic effect. There's an entire book to be written about

---

5. Joseph Goebbels, *Kampf um Berlin: der Anfang;* Alfred Rosenberg (1893–1946), *Der Mythus des 20. Jahrhunderts;* Gottfried Feder (b. 1883), *Kampf Gegen die Hochfinanz* and *Die Deutsches Staat;* Arthur Moeller van den Bruck (1876–1925), *Das Dritte Reich.*

"the art of manufacturing a leader." One would have to take apart Goebbels's and others' speeches and articles to see the Hitler myth slowly take shape and a vulgar human countenance attain divine majesty.

And look at these Brown stores! Oh, the enticing windows! Shirts and shorts, caps, insignias, satchels and rucksacks, and especially boots, belts, shoulder straps, and holsters. Everything that can disguise a man as a warrior is offered to lead the client into temptation. One may go without eating, but one buys a belt, if only to tighten it. If you are absolutely incapable of naming the thousand uniforms encountered every day, come into this boutique. You'll learn how to distinguish the old sa and ss uniforms from the new ones; you'll no longer confuse the Steel Helmet with the soldier of the Reichswehr, the auxiliary police with the young enlisted man of the Labor Service.

And the propaganda pursues you like a shooting pain. No sooner have you turned your eyes from the shop window than it succeeds in captivating you again. On the town hall, an enormous black eagle crushes some human figures in its claws. And you can read

> Crush Marxism,
> Death to Reaction:
> For this double defeat
> Revives our nation.

The victims of the eagle are, naturally, the Socialist and Communist *bonzes.* A little farther on, the Communist school is decorated with garlanded swastikas, and in Gothic lettering[6] the famous line from Schiller's *William Tell:* "We want to be a people united like brothers."

Elsewhere, in a very well designed public exhibition, you will be made to relive the history of the National Socialist party. You'll wait your turn—so numerous are the visitors and so great their piety—to bow over the venerable relics. Here is an autograph of the Führer; his hand passed over this paper . . . Uncover your head before this dusty sheet: it's the list, already thirteen years old, of the first party members in Munich. Despite the faded ink, you can still make out:

6. The Nazis revived the use of Gothic lettering, which they considered more authentically Germanic than Roman script.

No. 55: Hitler, Adolf: painter, Lothstrasse 29, born 20-4-89.

Don't think you can find any peace. If you want to have a *bock* in a beer hall, you'll have to listen to a performance of Guignol's *Weimar Republic* on the radio. It seems that the snoring that provokes such laughter is that of the Socialist deputies asleep on their benches. And if you ask to hear another program, you'll be treated to Hitler's latest harangue recorded and rebroadcast.

Finally, if you're exasperated and seek relief by trying to forget it all at the movies, *Bleeding Germany* will initiate you to the "national resurrection." It's 1914: flowers rain down upon the pointed-helmeted soldiers . . . Then, defeat: Scheidemann* on the balcony proclaiming the Republic: the Red hordes are masters of the streets. Versailles: rapacious hands tear strips off the Reich's flesh. The Passion continues. The Rhineland: the *Schwarze Schande* (black shame, i.e., the military occupation by Senegalese troops) and the invasion of the Ruhr. Then unemployment and the Great Depression: the Brown battalions begin to march . . . Hitler is holding forth with the gestures of a hysteric. Goebbels with the evil eyes of a hyena . . . finally, the apotheosis, the mad night of January 30, 1933: marching . . . marching . . . marching . . .

The Hitler Youth in the front rows, admitted at a reduced price, applaud wildly.

But next to me, my neighbor has fallen asleep.

5   *Horst Wessel and the Universe*

They didn't have their own hymn, and they couldn't very well steal the "Internationale." So they annexed—yet again—an old Communist melody, at once manly and tender, like so many popular German tunes.

Unlike the revolutionary proletariat, they had no heroes. To the pure image of the assassinated Karl Liebknecht, they had to counterpose an ersatz: millions of postcards would spread the legend of Horst Wessel.

This blond young "Aryan," whose adolescent face was displayed in every shop window, had two occupations during his lifetime, much like many of his comrades in arms: pimp and chief of a Storm Trooper section.

In February 1930, a rather obscure scuffle put him at odds with some rival; he remained on the ground. This dastardly deed was naturally attributed to the Communists, the young "Aryan" proclaimed a national hero, and three years later, with a stroke of the paintbrush, the Karl Liebknecht House, the headquarters of the Communist party, became the Horst Wessel House.

And since the robust lad had enjoyed writing new words for the Communist melody—a simple plagiarism of the old ones—the "Horst Wessel Song" was made the official hymn of the Third Reich:

Flag unfurled, ranks closed tight,
The SA advances, calm and firm.
The spirits of comrades, victims of the Red Front and Reaction,
March in our ranks . . .

But someone upset the celebration. The revolutionary writer Ilya Ehrenburg, with his characteristic verve, unmasked the young hero. The details contained in his article in *Izvestia* left no doubt as to the life-style of this Rouget de l'Isle of Berlin.[7] The article was translated into several languages. The affair threatened to take a nasty turn: try as one might to live in a sealed world, certain echoes from outside unpleasantly tickle the ears. A counteroffensive had to be organized, and quickly.

And so it was that a poster announcing a huge public rally appeared on the walls of Berlin. "Well-known foreign spokesmen" would speak on the theme "Horst Wessel and the Universe."

Let's pay our fifty pfennigs and breach the five-deep barrier of blond, booted, hand-picked ephebes. Let's take our places.

The Nail, a large cabaret, resembles any pleasure palace in the world. On ordinary days, one dines there at small tables to the sound of jazz. But this evening the stage is transformed into a tribune guarded by young flag-bearers standing at attention. An immense swastika-bearing red standard serves as a backdrop for the uniformed orchestra. Grouped around the small tables, the placid bourgeois are imbibing their *bocks* of beer with gestures that are already sluggish. There are many young Hitlerite girls in khaki vests. And naturally, lots of Siegfrieds in brown shirts, all dapper and moving about to the squeaking of leather.

A district chief who couldn't be much older than twenty opens the meeting, gives the Roman salute, and says in a curt, imperative voice: "If we authorize foreigners to speak in our meetings, it's because we can vouch for them: in fact, we will only let *National Socialist foreigners* speak [*sic*] . . ."

And after this reassuring exordium, he announces in a completely serious tone that the "Universe," indignant at the calumnies spread against the young hero, is going to rehabilitate Horst Wessel.

When he has finished, the first three rows of the honor guard do a regulation "Right!" and, in single file and at a quick pace, move toward one of the corners of the hall, where they break up. Throughout the evening, they will relieve their flag-bearing comrades who have remained motionless, like statues, at the foot of the podium.

After a Bulgarian general in civilian dress and with the hoarse voice of an

---

7. The sarcastic reference is to the composer of the French revolutionary march and national anthem, "La Marseillaise."

old soldier congratulates Hitler for saving the world from Bolshevism, a son of free America mounts the platform and is greeted with great flashes of magnesium. Paid by the German government to give a weekly radio propaganda talk to his compatriots, he thinks he's still in front of his microphone.

"Germany has awakened under the stewardship of a remarkable leader: Adolf Hitler . . . Horst Wessel is known and admired throughout the entire world . . ."

To vary the program a little, speaking choruses recite upon command the merits of the universal hero.

Then suddenly the temperature rises and the hall goes wild: an Italian in a black shirt, a flesh-and-blood Fascist! His chest covered with medals, injured twelve times during the war and almost as many times in the struggle against "Marxism," he scales the podium, freezes, and proclaims with arm outstretched, "Horst Wessel!"

And there he remains for a few moments, in direct communication with the departed.

The *signor* speaks in his mother tongue. We hear "*martire della causa sacra della rivoluzione* . . . will deliver the world *del pericolo rosso* . . ." At the end of each sentence, the German translation arouses enthusiasm.

When he has finished, the orchestra strikes up the anthem "Giovinezza,"[8] and the entire hall, on its feet and giving the Roman salute, takes up the chorus.

Finally, it's the turn of a tiny, timid, and sickly young man. From the very beginning of the evening, the comings and goings around him have intrigued me. Chiefs and under chiefs are falling all over each other to greet him. A great deal of importance is clearly attached to his presence and participation.

Everything becomes clear when "Mr. Akon Sneath, an alumnus of Oxford," is given the floor: In order to rehabilitate Horst Wessel, even the testimony of a British citizen is not forsaken.

The young man, who expresses himself in a correct German, explains that he was passing through Berlin for a few days, and that they insisted he speak: "I have accepted . . . But I can't tell you much about National

---

8. The anthem of Italian fascist youth, which begins "Giovinezza, giovinezza, primavera di bellezza" (Youth, youth, springtime of loveliness).

Socialism . . . For us, it's something that is really too difficult to understand . . . For we English, it's something so contrary to our entire history, to all our traditions . . . No, really, I can't say anything about it.

"As for Horst Wessel, of course we understand that a man may die for his ideals . . . whether this man be our friend *or our foe.*

"Ladies, gentlemen . . ."

A tiny salute and the British citizen vanishes from the podium on the tips of his feet.

To describe the consternation in the hall would be impossible. A few polite "bravos." A weighty silence. The district chief, boots resounding noisily, leaps precipitously onto the stage: "We hope that in the course of his stay in Germany Mr. Akon Sneath will come to understand our National Socialism. Moreover, in England there are many who have already come to familiarize themselves with it. National Socialism is no longer a German affair, but an international phenomenon!"

Of course it is, but from this point on, despite anything that may be said or sung, there are men and women in the hall touched by doubt . . .

The maître d'hôtel whispers in my ear, as if to try and reaffirm his faith: "Even if the Universe doesn't want to understand us, there will always be Italy."

6 *Death to the Mind*

They don't like intelligence, what Hitler calls "so-called intelligence." And wherever they encounter it, they pursue it, bind it to the stake, and deliver it to the flames.

Like everyone else, I'd read about this in the newspapers. It seemed unbelievable. It may have been possible in some land outside our universe, but not in the Germany of Goethe and Hegel . . .

And suddenly one morning, in front of the gate of a majestic university, I found myself before a kind of stake that had barely been hewn before being driven into the ground. Green-capped students, their faces streaked with gashes, were snickering.

Covers roughly torn off books were nailed to the post. Beautiful German books, so carefully produced and bound. I notice *All Quiet on the Western Front,* Ernst Glaeser's *Class of 1922,* Feuchtwanger's *The Jew Süss,* Emil Ludwig's *July 1914,* Jakob Wassermann's *The Maurizius Case.*[9]

Only a day earlier I had visited a library next to which our Bibliothèque nationale seemed poor and decrepit; a professional book-making school such as exists nowhere else in the world; a German booksellers' exhibition that would make our French publishers dream. How is one to understand?

Perhaps the young, refined, and cultured student who is sleeping in the bed next to mine this evening can explain it all to me. Disturbing the night's silence, I confide my confusion to him in a hushed voice: "When we speak together about philosophy or art, I know that we can understand

9. The first title, *Im Westen Nichts Neues,* by Erich Maria Remarque (1898–1970), is perhaps the best-known antiwar novel to emerge after the First World War. The other titles are Ernst Glaeser (1902–63), *Jahrgang 1902;* Lion Feuchtwanger (1884–1958), *Jud Süss. Roman;* Emil Ludwig (1881–1948), *Juli 1914;* Jakob Wasserman (1873–1934), *Der Fall Maurizius. Roman.*

each other, that we're from the same planet. But an instant later, you screw up your face, you pillory books that I love, you talk about drawing Jewish blood, and you sing absurd tunes like a drunken beast . . ."

My slightly rude candor doesn't displease him.

"I'm aware of everything you say, but I sing those absurd tunes *with pleasure.*"

There's a nuance of contempt in his intonation, something like the *credo quia absurdum,* or: "You French, you're too degenerate to understand."

And in the dark, pulling his blanket back up over his face, he whispers, along with his goodnight wishes, "Goebbels has said, 'Of course National Socialist propaganda is primitive. But the thinking of the people is primitive.'"

For a change of scene, here we are in the home of a young jurist, a friend and revolutionary. I don't doubt for a moment that he's remained faithful to his convictions. But what a strange decor! Fascist books on the table, on the bed, on the floor . . .

"What does it all mean? My poor friend, simply that I'm preparing for my law exams."

I think I have misunderstood.

"You understand perfectly. You know—or perhaps you don't—that our minister of justice in Prussia is that madman Kerrl, the one who proclaimed that in order to be a German judge one has to have understood the intimate essence of National Socialism. And so, these gentlemen are going to submit me to a five-hour interrogation on this *intimate essence.* And I'm getting ready for it."[10]

And as I'm too flabbergasted to respond, he adds: "If it would give you pleasure, I'll invite you to my baptism."

—"Your baptism?"

"Of course. Like many Germans, I was what they call a 'dissident,' in other words, a freethinker, since I'd left the Lutheran church. In order to become a functionary today, to take the exam, you have to belong to a confession: every day, thousands of people have to get baptized in order to

10. The Introduction discusses the Nazis' view of the law, and in particular the importance of the *Führerprinzip* in this regard.

keep earning their bread. The pastors can't handle it anymore. I will undergo a second interrogation, on the Holy Scriptures this time."

At this moment, his young brother, a schoolboy in shorts, enters: "Ludwig, go get your *Sacred History*"—for religious instruction is now compulsory at school.[11]

But I hadn't seen anything yet.

In a large square in Bremen, in the middle of a working-class district, not far from the People's House, a noisy group of children is milling about. What's going on? Let's join the onlookers.

Young boys, harnessed in leather, sleeves rolled up, are conscientiously piling up bundles of old papers and pamphlets with great strokes of the shovel and the broom. Strange ragmen indeed!

Over other people's shoulders, I try to examine these heaps of paper and make out some of the titles. And suddenly, my heart wrenched, I read *The Metalworker's Paper, The Bookworker*. And the Communist illustrated *AIZ*, the Socialist *Vorwärts*, pamphlets by Engels, and leaflets:

> Bremen the Red
> In distress,
> Demands work and bread!

And posters convening Social Democratic workers to mass meetings . . . Years of propaganda, of poverty, of struggle . . .

When the pyramid has attained the desired height, a kind of executioner prunes a wooden stick with a penknife and plants it at the summit. And greeted by the laughs and bravos of the Germanic *poulbots*,[12] he hoists a

---

11. For a chilling account of the teaching of religion in schools under the Nazis on the eve of the Second World War, see Erika Mann's *School for Barbarians* (82–91). "Every Roman Catholic class opens with the formula 'Heil Hitler! Blessed be Jesus Christ, in all Eternity, Amen,' [and] Protestant religious lessons . . . must emphasize 'that the existence of our people, in their racial peculiarity, has been willed by God and that it is an act of unfaithfulness toward God if racial values are not considered or if they are destroyed' " (83).

The 1945 edition adds: "And so the two brothers ironically sat down together over the same book and boned up on the story of the man from Galilee."

12. Montmartre street urchins. The 1945 edition uses the term *la marmaille*, (a horde of brats).

black shirt around this axis, an authentic black shirt from the Communist "defense groups." Then, with the self-satisfied care of the fetishist, he pins the red insignia of the Antifaschistische Aktion on the chest.

A ball of wrapping paper takes the place of a head; it's topped with the humble cap of a proletarian, worn and bent out of shape. I still don't understand.

"Thälmann, Thälmann!" suddenly shout the youngsters as they dance about with joy.

And now, under the effigy of the Communist leader, they unfurl a large strip of red fabric decorated with the three Socialist arrows. The unity these Communist and Socialist leaders never accomplished will be forged in the flames.

The preparations are finally done. To kill time, a boy searches at random in the pile, pulls out a book, and leafs through it: "Karl Marx," he chuckles, showing it to his neighbor. And then he throws it back with disgust and wipes his hands.

A few workers watch the spectacle, motionless and mute. I look them straight in the eyes: no tears, but something much more profound, a calm despair. But very quickly, they avert their eyes from my gaze.

The fire won't be lit until nightfall. An immense and silent crowd waits, pushed on despite itself by curiosity. At a quick pace, the ponderous Brown battalions succeed each other and take their places around the pyre. The green Steel Helmets are even more sluggish and more peasantlike. Finally the students, in full dress—Brandenburg-style pea jackets, multicolored scarves, fencers' lance and gloves, and the small toque—arrive to reassure themselves that the accursed doctrine has indeed perished in the flames.

A speech is broadcast over the loudspeakers, followed by the "Horst Wessel Song," and then, suddenly, a great flash of light rips open the night. In an instant, the effigy of Thälmann, the books, and the newspapers of the working class are nothing more than fireflies carried away by the wind.

Meager applause and then, already, as if ashamed of itself, the crowd quickly turns away from this auto-da-fé.[13]

13. 1945: "the crowd breaks up and flees the scene of the crime."

7   *Beware of the Jews!*

n Germany in 1933, the Jewish question is, for a foreigner, the easiest topic of conversation. It is best not to confess to being a Marxist before a random interlocutor, but raising the racial question with these crazed "Aryans" is much less risky.

With malicious pleasure, I pick at their weak spot and watch them writhe like impaled butterflies. After making some declaration of love for the German people . . .

"One owes the truth to a people one loves, let me tell you . . . a great savant like Einstein . . ."

My young blond *dolichocephal*[14] gives a start; his blue eyes fill up with red blood: "Einstein? *A dog!*"

Each time you try your hand at this little game, you'll obtain the same result: every throw wins.

In the common room of the hostel, an adolescent musician, so delicate when he passes his fingers over the guitar, deceives me for a moment. Not *him* . . . Nevertheless, I hazard the fatal name: now before me I have nothing less than a tiny rabid mongrel eager to bite.

"But after all, what have these unfortunate Jews done to you?"

"You want to know? Do you know that in Berlin, for example, seventy

---

14. The *Oxford English Dictionary* defines *dolicocephalic* as "long-headed: applied to the skulls of which the breadth is less than four-fifths (or, according to Broca, three-fourths) of the length" (1989, 4:936). Guérin uses the term sarcastically here to refer to Nazi race theory, according to which his interlocutor would possess the proper physical characteristics of a "pure Aryan."

percent of lawyers were Jewish?[15] What's the use of wasting years studying only to find them ensconced everywhere?"

Don't even try suggesting to him that this high percentage of lawyers was more to the honor of the Semites than the dishonor of the Germanic peoples; that if the profession is overcrowded, the fault is that of the capitalist crisis, not of the Israelites. You would be wasting your time.

"But your 'Aryan' race is only a myth!"

He draws himself up. "A myth? Look at me. Am I not, are we not, blond-haired Germanics? Unlike you French, we're of a pure race! And to defend ourselves, we won't hesitate to resort to *sterilization.*" This the young musician says with a frightening tenderness.

———

But let's take our leave of this barbarous youth and interrogate some adult "Aryans." Perhaps we'll meet more reasonable people.

While the barber glides his razor over my face, while the mechanic repairs my bicycle, while the innkeeper fills my *bock* with a foamy beer, let us slowly but surely steer the conversation.

"The Jews? Ah, my good man, we should have got rid of that ilk a long time ago. They're responsible for our misfortune. They came here to steal our bread. Look today and see if you can find a single one of them among the unemployed. Jobs for Germans first!"

How could 650,000 Jews[16] have deprived 65 million Germans of work? But when things go badly, a scapegoat is needed, and to spare the capitalists who are actually responsible from the people's wrath, the Israelites have been charged with all manner of sins.

Another man, a shopkeeper on the verge of bankruptcy, vents his hatred of the department stores upon me: "These Jewish bazaars, aren't they a disgrace? How can you struggle against the competition from these people? They were so ambitious that they're only an inch away from bankruptcy themselves."

15. In 1933, there were 3,030 Jewish lawyers and public notaries in Germany, or 16.6% of the total. Berlin had a disproportionate number of lawyers and civil servants by virtue of its role as capital city.

16. The figures of the Reich Statistical Office in 1933 show 503,000 Jews in Germany, or 0.76% of the total population. For additional statistics on Jewish presence in occupations, see Noakes and Pridham (1983:522–23).

You have to have heard these sons of the people who are not race theorists and who have never donned a brown shirt in order to grasp the wellsprings of their hatred. Hitler has invented nothing; he has simply listened, formulated, and guessed what an outlet anti-Semitism offers to the anticapitalist sentiment of the masses.

I retort, "Yes, but there are also lots of 'Aryans' among those who are devouring you . . ."

"We have to get rid of them, too."

Our good friend still has illusions.

"And the savants, as well, those famous intellectuals?"

He lowers his head. I sense he is suddenly less proud: "Of course, there have been some abuses . . . like in any revolution . . ." Then, he pulls himself together and his eyes fill with anger: "But we will never give in to the blackmail of international Jewry, to its *Greuelpropaganda* [its propaganda of atrocities]."[17]

And the struggle goes on just as determinedly, even when it's more hypocritical.[18]

The social insurance fund, which provides for over half of a German doctor's clientele, dismisses its Jewish practitioners; from those lawyers still practicing, certain procedures are taken away, such as judicial liquidations; public administrations exclude Jewish firms from their ordering; the industrials break all relations with intermediaries belonging to the accursed race; the National Socialist works cells foment strikes in businesses run by Jews and demand the dismissal of non-"Aryan" personnel; and the boycott of Jewish small businessmen pushes them slowly to the brink of disaster . . .

But I understood the true character of this struggle by opening a book that is a real provocation to murder. The title: *Jews Are Watching You.*[19] One would think it was an album of the anthropometric service. A certain number of well-known Jews are designated, by the publication of their

17. I.e., the publicizing by Jewish organizations abroad of acts of violence and persecution perpetrated against Jews in Nazi Germany, which served as the pretext for the boycott of Jewish businesses on April 1 (discussed in the Introduction).

18. 1945: "And the struggle continues, just as ferociously but more hypocritically, against the Israelites."

19. *Juden sehen Dich an.*

photographs, for public condemnation. And in the guise of a preface, one reads: "This gallery of corrupters of the people proves that none of these individuals has *until now* been executed by the National Revolution of 1933, even though their crimes cry out to highest heaven." For those who may not have understood, the names of yesterday's victims are followed, like that of Rosa Luxemburg,* by the caption "executed"; those of tomorrow's victims with the caption "not (yet) hanged."

Naturally, this blacklist includes several categories: first of all, the *bloodthirsty Jews:* from Rosa Luxemburg,* Bela Kun, and Trotsky to Professor Gumbel, driven from his chair at Heidelberg. Then come the *lying Jews:* Einstein, Hilferding, Stampfer, Emil Ludwig; the *swindler Jews:* those infamous sharks Barmat, Sklarz, Sklarek, etc. Then, the *corrupting Jews:* Professor Magnus Hirschfeld, the specialist of the sexual sciences, and Loewenstein, the inspiration of the Amis de l'enfance ouvrière,[20] which "taught children to despise the German people, race, and nation, and trained the children of the workers of Berlin to betray the people and submit to Jewish slavery." Now it's the turn of the *artist Jews,* among whom, next to the famous directors Piskator and Reinhardt, Charlie Chaplin is to be found! Finally, the *monied Jews:* the banker Jakob Goldschmidt and the Tietz brothers—the directors of the Berlin department store—round out the gallery; and the book ends with these words: "The fight isn't over, the fight goes on! Heil Hitler!"[21]

But to satisfy my conscience I must nevertheless evoke another image: In a well-to-do bourgeois interior, an Israelite family welcomes me. Lamenting and bewailing the unimaginable circumstances that have rent its gentle quietude, its honorable existence, its assured revenues, they ask, "Can you advise us? Should we go to France? Can we live in Palestine?"

Behind the image of this slightly corpulent bourgeois, I perceive the shadow of the wandering Jew, walking stick in hand, once again taking to the road . . .

Eyes full of tears, his wife explains: "If you only knew, Monsieur, how German I feel! We were living in America. I forced my husband to come back here. What have we done to be treated this way?"

20. Literally, "Friends of Working-Class Childhood," a children's relief fund.
21. The account of this book in *The Brown Terror* notes that several individuals who would be considered non-Jews even according to the Nazis' own race theory are included in the volume; among them is Karl Liebknecht,* a descendant of Martin Luther! (235–36).

Why, oh why did she have to add, "After all, this new regime, we would accommodate ourselves to it, if only it would leave us alone."[22]

The charm is suddenly broken. I think about those who, Jewish or non-Jewish, have been hungry for years; about those who, Jewish or non-Jewish, are rotting today in the Brown prisons.

22. Klaus Mann was shocked by the naïveté of some Jews who tried to accommodate themselves to the new regime: "It was profoundly irritating to see Jewish book reviewers all in raptures, say, about the sinister autobiography of a certain Ernst von Salomon—one of the dashing young men, incidentally, who participated in the assassination of a truly great German Jew, [the Weimar foreign minister] Walther Rathenau. Out of 'objectivity' and masochism, these perverse intellectuals politely analyzed and heartily encouraged their own murderers" (1942:231).

8   *War or Peace?*

The Hitlerite drama is coupled with another that is no less formidable, and which affects us more directly: that of Franco-German relations.

If you wish to understand, go into any of the two hundred theaters in Germany where they are presently performing Hanns Johst's *Schlageter*. This Schlageter, today a national hero to the same degree as Horst Wessel, was a sad specimen. He signed up just after the war for the infamous *corps francs*[23] in the East, then was a spy in the service of Poland. He showed up again in 1923 during the invasion of the Ruhr Valley both as an informer for France and as a saboteur for Germany. In March, he blew up a railway bridge; on May 26, the French occupation troops shot him.

But if the man hardly deserves pity, his execution became a symbol: Schlageter incarnates the resistance to Poincaré's *coup de force*.[24] For ten years, National Socialism has been able to draw the yeast for its prodigious ascent from this story.

23. The German Free Corps, groups of "volunteer" soldiers who, following Germany's demilitarization at the end of World War I, were organized by Kurt von Schleicher. He would later immediately precede Hitler as chancellor. Konrad Heiden explains: "The outward pretext for the forming of this army was the communistic revolts in several parts of the Reich. . . . Even the Allies for a short time tacitly agreed with this revival of the German army. For with them, too, there was fear of Communism" (243).

24. Raymond Poincaré served as president of the French Republic until 1920. In 1922, he returned to political life as premier. Not yet satisfied that Germany's militaristic will had been broken, he used the unresolved issue of the extent of German reparation payments as a pretext for sending the French army to occupy the Ruhr Valley, Germany's industrial heartland, on January 11, 1923. The occupation was met with a mass strike and a nearly complete shutdown of all production facilities.

"We belong to Schlageter because he is the first soldier of the Third Reich!" cries one of the characters in the play.

And Schlageter himself explains: "We have the right—the French have given it to us through their occupation—to rise up and say: *Entente, fraternization, internationale* of peoples, all of this was merely charlatanism! And so, for a radically national government! To hell with the system[25] of November 1918!"

And while the "hero" prepares his assault, the tragic opposition between the old socialist generation and the fascist new one is drawn: the son of a Social Democratic senior functionary is going to lend Schlageter his utmost assistance.

In vain the father—whom the author fails to make ridiculous—speaks of "exterminating through fire and sword the last adventurers, fanatics, firebrands, and bandits of the world war." In vain he implores, "We want peace! It is I who tell you this, my son, I who was under fire for four years . . ."

The public begins to get nervous. Around me, I hear stifled sobs.

The curtain comes up for the last time: a French firing squad in sky blue uniforms is binding Schlageter to the post.

"Germany," cries the condemned man, "a final word, a wish, an order . . . Germany, awake! Ignite! Blaze!"

A horrible crackling. Then silence and night. When light returns to the hall, tears are flowing.

"And soon the French will invade us again!" screams a woman near me, as if mad.

[The following passage appears in the 1945 edition:

The evil seeds that had been sown slowly germinated: those "marvelous flowers of hatred," as a German orator put it in 1923, blossomed. Today, after German schoolchildren bellow out their fascist hymns, they learn from the example of this saboteur of the Ruhr. Take, for example, this small composition that merited the student who wrote it the highest mark. I was able to transcribe it directly from the notebook:

25. The term used to describe the terms of Germany's capitulation in the First World War, and eventually used by the Nazis to describe the entire period during which Germany lived under the terms of the Treaty of Versailles (i.e., *der Systemzeit*).

Schlageter's Last Act

Darkest night. From out there, a rustling of bodies brushing against each other. Human forms slither rapidly along the railway line. It's Schlageter and his men. A searchlight skims the night. "Get down!" Schlageter orders. Glued to the ground, they crawl along until they reach the ballast. Schlageter takes the package of dynamite from his pocket, places it on the rails, lights the fuse with the end of his cigarette, and then, followed by his men, turns around and retreats.

As soon as they are out of the searchlight's range, they leap up and break into a run. From out there, an explosion rips through the silence. A satisfied smile brightens Schlageter's face: mission accomplished!]

As in our own country, a generation will soon reach maturity without having known the horrors of war.

You have to have heard those young people whom you ask innocently, "Do you play sports?" respond in an angry and curt tone, "*Kein sport! Wehrsport!*"[26]

You have to have seen them exhaling voluptuous "Ahs!" at the sight of the Reichswehr waddling madly about on parade to the goose step.

Today, a generation is openly preparing itself. Freed of compulsory military service, it finds it amusing to play soldier by marching along the highways, pack on the back, advancing as if for skirmishes, hugging the ground on exercise fields, and banging old pots to alert the urban population to air attacks.

However, the suffering endured during the 1914–18 war remains vivid in the memory of the German people. Accompany me to a small village pub where men and women are gathered around a loudspeaker in silent anticipation. At three o'clock, the Führer will speak to the world from his

---

26. "No sports! Military training!" (lit., "defensive sport"). Erika Mann cites a 1933 *Handbook for Hitler Youth* that includes a *Wehrsport* curriculum, a large part of which is "related to 'peaceful sport' [such] as the throwing of bombs." Marching formed a major component of such "sport," with fifteen-year-olds, for example, marching 13.5 miles a day with an eleven-pound load. In over a third of military conscripts, such excesses produced an epidemic of flat feet, "the trait which, apart from large noses and full lips, is most used in anti-Semitic caricatures!" (119).

tribune at the Reichstag. But thanks to the magic of radio, you would think he had come in person to this very inn for an intimate chat.

Listen to him vaticinate: "No war in Europe could create something better to replace what exists . . . If such madness happened one day, it would be the ruin of the social order, a chaos without end . . ."

Observe the "Ja . . . ja's," the nodding heads of your neighbors.

And the medium with the beady, bulging eyes prepares an easy success for himself with this argument: "Germany would be ready to dissolve all its military organizations and destroy all its remaining arms if others, without exception, did the same. Germany doesn't ask to rearm, but calls on other states to disarm!"

Of course, I say to myself, the man is speaking in bad faith; it's too easy to seize upon the pretext so generously furnished by the Western powers: by not disarming, despite their undertaking to do so at Versailles, they have played, and continue to play, into his hands.

The evening following this speech, an old woman, tears in her eyes, comes toward me and pleads with all her soul: "My husband fell there, in your country . . . Do you hear? We don't want war."

Fine, but watch out that soon this old German woman doesn't herself become enraged!

We're heading straight toward 'National Bolshevism,'" I heard many times during my trip.[27]

What is this new disease? The expression, you will tell me, is as incorrect as it is dangerous. Incorrect because Bolshevism and nationalism (at least until the day when the German Communist party, too, began to try and outbid others with the nationalist card) are theoretically antinomical. Dangerous, because it gives credence to the lie of a possible marriage between these two opposites.

But inappropriate as it may be, it conveys a mood that is growing among the masses. To learn more about this, let us go deep into their humble abodes.

On the road, I meet the son of a carpenter from Moabit, a young unemployed vagabond, a Red whose eyes shine when you speak to him of Thälmann, of "Teddy." I don't know why, but I supposed that the father, too, was a Communist. And his coarse proletarian speech and revolutionary arguments deceive me for a moment:

"You see, we workers have been betrayed by the two workers' parties. They should have forged unity in action. They didn't want to." Then, suddenly, this suspect argument: "Now we have to save ourselves."

27. At the end of World War I, "National Bolshevism" became a call for communism in Germany without the internationalist element. This call was particularly fueled by the French occupation of the Ruhr Valley in 1923. "Theorists" of National Bolshevism included Arthur Moeller van den Bruck and Otto Strasser. National Bolshevist currents existed in other European countries, as well. These tended everywhere to be right wing and populist in tone. Lenin's *"Left-Wing" Communism: An Infantile Disorder* was directed at such deviations from Communist internationalism.

"*Ourselves?*"

"The German people! We've had enough of being humiliated, of being treated like slaves. Enough of paying taxes for war tribute . . ."

And when I object that outside of revolutionary internationalism there is no salvation: "Yes, yes . . . the International, that's all very nice. Once, we sent millions of gold marks to the English miners when they were on strike. But how have they helped us in return?"

And after filling his pipe: "We'll have to make our revolution alone. While waiting for the International to exist, we have to think about the present. First of all, to liberate ourselves from the *Diktat* of Versailles, to free our oppressed comrades in Silesia, in the Saarland, in Austria, in the Sudentenland, in Memel and Dantzig . . . to found a German workers' state!"[28]

There are thousands like him, mixing up their confused demands for socialism with a fanatical sentiment born of national humiliation. And it is more so among the youth than the adults. Let's sit at the roadside beside a pedestrian who, pack on his back, is heading for a "voluntary labor camp." When he starts praising discipline that is freely consented to and the virtues of cheap labor, he makes me so angry that I have to restrain myself from attacking him on the spot.

But suddenly, as if animated by a spring, he lets his mask fall and shares his secret with me: "Don't you see, I've been a National Socialist for years . . . one of those who, in 1928, gave a sound thrashing to the Rhenish separatists. Today, I quit the party."

"Why?"

"Because I'm not satisfied. It's no longer a revolutionary party, it hasn't got any teeth. I want *real socialism.* For fourteen years, the Social Democratic party had the chance to build it, but what did it do about it? I'm not a Communist, because I'm a German first and I don't want to be treated like a Russian *moujik,* but I respect the Communists and feel closer to them than the rest."

He speaks to me hatefully of the rich, the magnates of industry, the large

28. The speaker here refers to the conviction that there exists a "Greater Germany" beyond the boundaries of the Reich.

landowners. And with a sigh: "So long as they all betray socialism, I will remain without a party."

"National Bolshevism." What better term to translate these desperately ambivalent aspirations?

Let's go further. Let's forget who we are. Let's slide in among the Brownshirts. Let's try to intercept the thoughts hidden behind their "Heil Hitler!"'s.

Saturday evening at a popular dance hall in a working-class district of Leipzig. Men and women around tables, dressed like petit bourgeois, like all German workers. There are many SA's and Hitler Youth, but here there is neither arrogance nor starchiness; it's free and easy, noisy laughter—we're among the people. The orchestra, in uniform, plays good classical music: Wagner, Verdi. At the intermission, an orator mounts the stage and harangues the crowd, which is at first attentive and docile. The theme: "Our Revolution."

"Our Revolution, *Volksgenossen,*[29] has only begun. We haven't yet attained any of our goals. There's talk of a national government, of a national awakening. . . . What's all that about? It's the *Socialist* part of our program that matters."

The crowd emits a satisfied "Ah!" This is what everyone was thinking but didn't dare articulate. Now their gaze passionately follows this man who speaks for them all.

"The Reich of Wilhelm II was a Reich without an ideal. The bourgeoisie ruled with its disgusting materialism and its contempt for the proletariat. The 1918 Revolution, *Volksgenossen,* couldn't destroy the old system. The Socialist leaders abandoned the dictatorship of the proletariat for the golden calf. They betrayed the nation and they betrayed the people. As for communism, it's proven itself unable to get rid of them, since Stalin renounced Leninist Bolshevism for capitalist individualism."

I listen spellbound to this tirade. Am I really at a Hitlerite meeting? But the demagogue knows what he's doing, for the crowd is vibrating around me at an ever-increasing rhythm.

29. "National comrades"; i.e., those considered by Nazi ideology to be legitimately included in the German nation. Others were situated at various points along a continuum as *Gemeinschaftsfremde,* or "community aliens" (Peukert, 220–22).

"The bourgeoisie, *Volksgenossen,* continued to monopolize patriotism, to abandon the masses to Marxism, that dog's breakfast. For our part, we've understood that we had to go to the proletariat and enter into it, that to conquer Germany meant conquering the working class. And when we revealed the idea of the Fatherland to these proletarians, there were tears of gratitude on many a face . . ."

This emphatic missionary language is followed by diatribe and threats: "We have now but one enemy to vanquish: the bourgeoisie. Too bad for it if it doesn't want to give in, if it doesn't want to understand . . ."

And carried away by his eloquence, he lets the admission slip out: "Besides, one day it will be grateful that we treated it this way."

But the crowd didn't hear that. It believes only that the revolution has begun, that socialism is on the horizon. And when he has finished, it sings with raw anger:

> O producers, you deeply suffer
> The poverty of the times.
> The army of the unemployed
> Relentlessly grows.
>
> But joyous and free worker,
> Still you sing the old song:
> "We are the workers,
> The Proletariat!"
>
> You labor every day
> For a salary of famine.
> But the Tietzs, the Wertheims, and the Cohns
> Know neither poverty nor pain.
> You exhaust and overwork yourself:
> Who benefits from your labor?
> It's the shareholders,
> The Profitariat.
>
> . . . Now sunder your chains,
> German worker!
> Moscow cannot save you
> No more than the "Socialos"!
> Of the Israelites you are a slave!

Be it Soviet star or *bonzes'* glitter,
You remain the serf
Of the Profitariat!

The International
Has been a fine help indeed!
But the light of German freedom
Now shines on the horizon.

I have never heard people sing with such faith. Never have I seen, even among the Aissaouas of Islam, people so projected out of themselves. I am lost on my feet, motionless in the middle of this mass that would die without interrupting its song.

Already the rumor is spreading that the Storm Trooper sections are getting impatient, even mutinous. I think to myself that soon it will be necessary to satisfy this crowd—or else crush it brutally.

10 The Swastika over the Trade Unions

Just after May Day, the workers' holiday during which the Führer celebrated *"the proletarian idealism which alone makes possible the life and existence of all,"* the regime took possession of the trade unions.[30]

I arrived in Germany just as these events were taking place. With emotional curiosity, I went back to look at the handsome buildings with their audaciously modern architecture, next to which our *Bourses du travail* would look like poor relatives. Barely a few months after my last year's visit, this immense organization, our comrades' pride, had been swallowed up by fascism. Today, swastika flags hang from the windows and on the façade, the inscription People's House has given way to another, The House of German Labor, daubed across garish banners.

At the doors, workers press against each other, silently reading the conqueror's posters and newspapers. I mingle with them and try to read their faces, but I detect only a mute stupor.

What has happened? A comrade who lived through the events day by day, who saw the catastrophe coming, explains—and I transcribe:

"You see, when you come down to it this imposing 'fortress' had many fissures . . . a Colossus with feet of clay, as you say. As long as the conjuncture was favorable, everything was fine. With dues from seven million members, we threw ourselves into building these magnificent—and overly luxurious—edifices. We believed in eternal prosperity; we believed in good

---

30. In the 1945 edition, section 10 is entitled "Up Against the Wall" and deals with the economic contradictions faced by the Nazi regime. It is entirely omitted from the current version. "The Swastika over the Trade Unions" is section 11 in the 1945 edition, which has eighteen sections in all.

Precisely, the trade unions were taken over on May 2, 1933.

faith that within the system we could achieve that *economic democracy* so dear to the heart of the theoretician Naphtali.[31] Then came the Depression. Several million members, out of work, deserted the organizations. To others, we had to distribute a great deal of unemployment relief. The unions' main weapon, the strike, became too risky. And then, fascism was born. Our leaders, who hadn't known how to adapt to the Depression, knew no more about how to confront Hitler. Against an aggressive adversary, you can't just fight with flowery proclamations and handsome buildings. Do you know the splendid trade union school at Bernau, a kind of Thélème Abbey?"[32]

"Yes, I visited it last year, and not without a certain malaise . . ."

"Well, Bernau embodied our trade unionism along with everything it was lacking, by which I mean a soul and a will to struggle. Too often our organizations were merely cooperative banks. The worker came here to get his due just like at the social insurance office or the unemployment bureau. Not the slightest revolutionary ideal: nothing but a bureaucratic attitude. Look, I don't want to deprecate the past work of the German trade unions. I know only too well what they've done for the emancipation and the culture of our proletariat . . ."

"They succeeded in organizing the masses, which is certainly something!"

"Yes, but by forgetting about their *popular* character . . . The ADGB wound up becoming a cog of the state. Corporatism, syndicalism, and collaboration led straight to fascism. From slogans like "general interest" and "managed economy" to Hitlerite phraseology is only a small step. I would add that the Communists bear their share of responsibility with the slogan "Desert the reformist unions!" Then we come to the last few months—under the pretext of saving what they believed could be saved, they groveled before the conqueror; they slid down a continuous and

31. In the 1945 edition, a note identifies Naphtali as "a trade union theoretician, and author of a book by this title."

32. The reference is to Rabelais's novel, *Gargantua* (1534), in which the giant's companion, Frère Jean des Entommeures, is given the abbey as a reward for his accomplishments on the battlefield. Following the precept "Fay ce que tu voudras" (Do what you will), Thélème is a community of men and women who live harmoniously and devote themselves to the judicious cultivation of mind and body.

imperceptible slope; the worker, lulled by this tactic, didn't see the decisive moment approaching.

"One morning, it was enough to send a few young Brownshirts armed with bludgeons into the People's Houses and the porters hid under their beds, like in Leipzig. On the balcony, the Brownshirts unfurled a swastika flag, and the magnificent palace of the ADGB became the headquarters of Dr. Ley* and his so-called Labor Front [DAF*].[33] 'The payment of benefits is guaranteed!' proclaimed fascism, and the administrative machinery continued to function as before. Thus were the trade unions *gleichgeschaltet,* or 'brought into conformity,' as they say."[34]

My interlocutor shows me one of the innumerable hastily printed brochures in which the Nazis, going through the books of the unions, take the *bonzes* to task: "At least fifty percent of it is lies. Unfortunately, though, they left themselves wide open for some of the attacks. There's not as much corruption as they claim, but there is a tendency to live too well. As for the new team, I can assure you they won't be giving lessons in asceticism!"

Continuing my investigation, I went to visit a trade union militant whom I had met the year before. As access to the People's Houses is prohibited to the profane, I had to wait in the street. Powerful limousines with swastika pennants, not very proletarian at all, stop in front of the door. "Commissioners" get out—brown shirts, boots, belts—while the uniformed orderlies click their heels and come to attention. Finally, my friend arrives, shows his pass to the SA, for you can't leave the building without authorization, and smiles at me sadly: "And so, you see what's become of us . . ."

"And you can stay?"

"I'm dismissed as of the first of September. The smart alecks say that

33. Dr. Robert Ley's instructions for the "coordination" of the unions are reproduced in Noakes and Pridham, doc. 220 (330–31).
34. For a fuller discussion of *Gleichschaltung,* see the Introduction. With specific reference to the takeover of the unions, Konrad Heiden recounts that in Berlin the leaders Leipart and Grassman "were beaten, forced to run long distances and do knee-bends; the same occurred all over the Reich with such oppressive uniformity that for the first time the German public learned the full meaning of 'co-ordination.' In paralyzed wonder, the overpowered workers looked on at their own ruin" (600).

we'd always promised to return to the rank and file, and that they'll renew the cadres by drawing from the 'base.' They're keeping us on these few months so that we can train them. But it's not easy! We're working in the atmosphere of a guardhouse. I have armed young men in my office; we're spied on from morning until evening, and the 'commissioners' spend their time collecting misdemeanor slips on us."

"And where do these infamous commissioners come from?"

"From all over. Many *Akademiker,* intellectuals, lawyers, who know nothing about labor problems. Former secretaries of yellow or Christian unions . . . old turncoats of our own, like Winnig, who used to be the secretary of the Building Trades Federation . . . and even much more recent turncoats. For we, too, have our budding fascists."

I couldn't help but think of that Herr Doktor I visited last year at the ADGB and who today proclaims that the national government alone is "capable of achieving socialism."

But it's time for my interlocutor to go back to work. He sighs, taking me by the arm: "Did I ever tell you that once, many years ago, I was a Communist? I was expelled for being soft on Leipart's 'reformism.' Today, I see everything clearly: even if I don't approve of the disastrous split tactic of the Red unions, I too was mistaken, grievously mistaken."

He is so upset that I hold myself back from twisting the knife in the wound. "And now, what are you going to do? How are you going to live?"

He made a vague gesture of a man without hope. "How am I going to live? I was a gasworker, but of course the gas company won't take me back. I can't open a business: a recent law, aimed at us, prohibits the issuing of new licenses. All that's left are the 'great public works,' in other words, forced labor!"

Once the first moment of stupor had passed, the masses pulled themselves together. If some have been mollified by the continued payment of benefits, others react and demand that trade union democracy be respected. They're not the least bit disposed to hold their tongues and stand at attention listening to the Führer's speeches. They demand that their leaders be elected.

In Leipzig, during a meeting of the Central Federation of Employees, a

Socialist member courageously asks for the floor, lists his grievances, and is met with lively applause. Precipitously, the meeting is adjourned.

In Kiel, the workers go on strike to protest the dismissal of their shop-floor delegates. In Hamburg, the Nazi leaders denounce the "corrupt *bonzes*" during an assembly. "Very well!" respond those in attendance, "let's name a commission of inquiry." But the assembly is immediately dissolved.

And so the Nazis have become timid. They lose their self-assurance and blush before these demanding crowds. And rather than confronting them, they prefer to abstain from all contact.

In the library of a People's House, an SA enters brusquely and shouts a formidable *"Heil Hitler!"* Many workers are busy reading. Nobody responds, nobody budges. After a stiff moment of surprise, the youth leaves without asking anything more.

Nevertheless, they haven't yet completely given up trying to win over the workers. And nobody is as skilled at it as Dr. Robert Ley. *Lévy,* say the backbiters, and this frenzied racist does have the most pronounced of what are taken to be typical Semitic features. The man has a past: A great lover of kirsch, it was he who delicately planted an empty bottle on the skull of the Social Democratic leader Wels in a Cologne beer hall.

"As for myself," he insists in his proclamations to the workers, *"I am a poor son of a peasant and know what poverty is. I spent seven years in one of the largest plants in Germany and know all about exploitation by anonymous finance capital."*

In fact, when Mr. Ley decided to quit I. G. Farben, the infamous paint corporation,[35] he received an indemnity of ten thousand gold marks in cold cash.

And to slowly but surely endear himself to the masses, the head of the Labor Front has distributed over four million copies of the *Arbeitertum,* a magnificent illustrated newspaper. Along with advertisements for Hitler and profound slogans such as "The class struggle and the prejudices of social status are done away with" or "Honor labor," he deploys the artifices of his seduction.

"My dear *Volksgenossen,*" the siren begins, "you say to us [I am translating word for word]: 'What more could you want? Isn't absolute power already yours?' Of course we have power, but we haven't yet won over the

---

35. During the Second World War, I. G. Farben used slave labor from the concentration camps, including Auschwitz, next to which it had a plant.

whole people. You workers still aren't with us one hundred percent, and it's precisely you we want. We shall not rest until you have made a well-informed decision to join with us for good."

And as the honest proletarian remains reticent at the other end of the sofa, an arm is draped around his neck: "*Of course we know that deep down you are still a Marxist trade unionist and that you will read this issue of the* Arbeitertum *with mixed feelings. Such a sudden change may well have taken you by surprise. Perhaps you are still convinced that our takeover of the union halls and the federations was a* coup de force *against workers' rights. Nothing could be further from the truth!*"

Our temptress explains maternally that she merely wanted to save her good union friend from the clutches of the evil *bonzes,* that the wheels of the organization will be simplified and the people's pennies saved. And when the proletarian tries to escape her advances: "*We're not asking you to become a National Socialist today. To understand what we're about, you'll need more time than that. But one day, we're sure you'll admit in all fairness that when we kicked out your* bonzes, *it was the eleventh hour. We know that eventually you will agree with us . . . for we will command your confidence.*"

Undoubtedly, this alluring talk made some weaker heads spin. But proletarian common sense isn't so easily ravished.

And when it seems that Dr. Ley's seduction may not work, Hitler himself is called to the rescue.

"Throughout the years he was struggling for power," explains the *Arbeitertum* to its readers, "the Führer learned to recognize the loyalty of the modest man behind his plow or leaning over his workbench. As he silently did his duty as a pioneer of labor for five years as a construction worker and cement mixer, and then for a second time as an unknown soldier for four years at the front in the Great War, he lived, worked, and fought with workers."

And the new Messiah offers himself as an "honest broker" between Capital and Labor.

"I believe," he states, "that destiny has chosen me for this role. I have no personal interest in it. I depend neither on the state, nor on the public service, nor on the economy, nor industry, nor on a trade union. I am an independent man. Nothing would make me prouder than to be able to say at the end of my life, 'I brought the German workers to the German Reich'!"

On May 16, Dr. Ley, "in the name of Labor," signed an armistice with his crony Wagener, "in the name of Capital." A two-month economic truce has come into effect, during which union rates will be protected and strikes strictly prohibited. And as the "honest broker" can't be everywhere at once, "surrogates" will represent him in every large region and will decide without right of appeal in matters of social conflict, regulate salaries, and set contracts.

"We will obtain good rates for you to the extent that the currently catastrophic situation of the German economy allows," the *Arbeitertum* admits in the end.

And if the worker fears he has misunderstood: "Hitler demands obedience . . ."

But impatience is growing among the ranks of the Brownshirts. The scoundrels are caught at their own game; to show that they're as "revolutionary" as the Communists, they've created National Socialist Works Cells (NSBO). Solemnly, they recognize the right to strike and have distributed a flood of demagogic brochures against the "selfish" big bosses. And now that the people have won, the worthy proletarians in the cells really want to see the "revolution" carried onto the shop floor.

Initially, the Nazis wavered and didn't quite know what to do with the unions. They deluded themselves by forming the NSBO into a new cooperative organization. Many Socialist and Communist workers were forcibly enrolled in the cells, while others skillfully infiltrated them. Now, all of these elements are restless.

Incident follows upon incident: Cell delegates bang their fists on the boss's desk demanding control over the business or the reduction of top salaries and high-ranking personnel. Others recall that Goebbels had promised to cancel the wage-slashing Brüning decrees once the Nazis were in power. But such resistance is ruthlessly broken, the "ringleaders" thrown out of the factory, expelled, and replaced by safer elements. It is estimated that soon the NSBO will be rid of some 100,000 undesirables and will regain its character as a tested political faction.

But the current is so strong that ballast has to be dumped. So, from time to time, "bad" bosses who lay off workers or who don't respect the rates are arrested for "economic sabotage" and sent to a concentration camp for twenty-four hours. In return, things in the plant simmer down for a while.

But how easy it remains to fluster a young Nazi trade unionist! In conclusion, consider this short discussion:

"The right to strike wasn't an invention of the politicians; it was your only weapon. How are you going to defend your wages now?"

At first, my interlocutor seems sure of himself: "The state will protect them . . ."

"Yes, but the big shots have bigger mouths. They'll always have more influence than you over the state."

The argument gets to him. I sense him caught off guard, worried. And so he clings desperately to this last hope: "I have confidence in Hitler."

"The man isn't eternal. And when Hitler's no longer there?"

He looks at me stunned, suddenly face-to-face with the void.

12 *The Other Germany*

If we've been a bit tardy in visiting our friends and seeing what life is like in the other Germany, it's because an abyss wider than a frontier and deeper than an ocean separates it from the first. "Unification of the people!" proclaims fascism. In fact, never has this country been divided into two more irreconcilable camps.

Here, on a gray, rainy day, then, is that other Germany along the highway between Cologne and Dusseldorf. Imagine two young unemployed men walking together, bare-legged with worn-down boots, hair curling over their necks, and a few long black whiskers protruding from their emaciated chins.

"Ah! You're French! It's not possible!"

Their eyes light up. Finally, someone they can talk to without fearing an informer. And when they learn of my opinions, they happily pull the insignia of the Communist party out of their coat lining.

"For the moment, we are beaten. It will take time, but there's no doubt of the final outcome."

With a jolt of the back, they adjust the position of their rucksacks and exclaim in a tone of ferocious determination, "They won't get us with their forced labor!"

I watch the poor waifs as they once again take to the endless highway. Motorcyclists, proud and provocative in their brown uniforms, brush against them as they pass. Unlike these victors of the day, they don't have handsome uniforms. They're shabby, but defiant.

A little farther along in the Ruhr Valley, it's another rainy day as sad as death. Smokeless chimneys and their sleeping furnaces, the gray of the cobblestones, of the houses, of the sky—everything conveys a sorrowful impression of emptiness and distress. I go into a village *bistrot* to have a bite to eat.

Some young workers in blue caps, hunched over, talk in low voices. One of them comes to sit at my table. Stating my nationality, I ask him, just for something to say, whether unemployment is still so rampant. "Alas!" he sighs. And in the hollow of my ear: "And it won't improve with the new government!" This suffices. We understand each other.

Thus, the foreigner can open many hearts in this terrorized Germany. As soon as people know who I am, the confidences begin. A worker in a bookstore, after a few moments of conversation, passionately tells me of his hatreds and his hopes. When we are alone in the back room, a waiter in a restaurant announces almost point-blank: "You're French? Monsieur, I am a Communist!"

And in a youth hostel where young Nazis have been cynically bragging to me about the riding crop as a means of persuasion, a big fellow takes me aside as if wishing to console me: "Don't lose confidence. Universalist Germany, Goethe's Germany, we'll see it again!"[36]

But here is the purest of all these images. Perhaps also the most fugitive and fragile. All the young *Wandervögel*[37] who are at the dormitory tonight belong to the other Germany. All are unemployed and transient musicians.[38] From their guitars hang bunches of multicolored ribbons. No shoulder straps imprison their loose-fitting azure vests.

And after making sure that the doors and windows are closed, that

36. The 1945 edition adds: "It will be a socialist Germany!"

37. Literally, "birds of passage." "The movement started in 1896 as a small group of Berlin schoolboys given to camping trips, treks through the country in colorful, traditional clothes, the strict avoidance of women, and occasional smoking, drinking, and sex. By 1906, the Wandervögel had spread over Northern Germany, and in 1907, a Southern branch began operations with a somewhat different orientation: separate but equal women's groups were encouraged, abstinence from tobacco, sex, and alcohol was demanded" (Steakley, 54–55). See also Becker (1946) and Laqueur (1984).

38. In the 1945 edition, this paragraph begins: "O happiness! These young *Wanderer* who find themselves in the dormitory tonight are all comrades, all unemployed and traveling musicians. Charming vestiges of the age of Werther, what are you doing in the century of Horst Wessel? Their fanciful skullcaps would give them an ecclesiastical look if it weren't for the large bird feathers planted in them."

nobody indiscrete is listening, they sing in accompaniment to the old proletarian melodies, "Brothers Toward the Sun," "The Free Road," using the old words since deformed and banned.

Gentle bohemians who love only freedom, you are no longer at home in your own country. As you have told me yourselves: "They're going to hunt down the musicians and the beggars without mercy. They're going to throw us into their labor camps, bend us to their discipline, try to transform us under their knout."

Already, the enemy has entered the dormitory with a ghastly squeaking of leather. Just as suddenly, you stopped singing. Now you are conversing in low voices. And in the shadows, watching from their bunks, the Brown warriors spy on you.

[The following appears in the 1945 edition:

Soon, the nightingale will be mute in its cage; in Werther's Germany, only the sound of boots will be heard.

.　.　.　.　.

Here, sun pours in through all the open windows and sheds its light on the walls. This crèche is the good work of a few frail young women. Here, children of alcoholic or syphilitic workers are surrounded with maternal tenderness: their innocent and rosy heads rest sleeping on white pillows. But these young women are revolutionaries; they no longer have the right to devote themselves to such work; the crèche is dissolved.

And doting over the toddlers who are about to be torn away from them, these young women of *the other Germany* remind me of Hitler's terrible promise: "We will take their children from them."

.　.　.　.　.

But they can't force their way into every home.

There, far from suspicious glances and informers, lives the Germany we love.

Let's ring at the door . . .]

Let's ring at a friendly door. A long silence, then the sound of muffled steps. From behind a kind of glass peephole, a worried eye observes us: If it's the enemy, one needs time to light the gas and destroy illegal papers and tracts.

We are welcomed into a handsome lodging that many French workers could only dream of. At the threshold, this teacher who has just been dismissed for his Socialist ideas confides: "Yes, we're well housed! We'll get 312 francs unemployment relief per month, plus a 60-franc housing indemnity . . . and the rent is 360 francs! We'll have 12 francs left for our two children and ourselves. And right now is a hell of a time to try and find a cheaper apartment!"

So as not to feel the hollow in their stomachs, they live at a slowed-down pace: prolonged sleep in the morning followed by long siestas on the sofa in the afternoon. They take their time reading the newspaper—the stupid, empty, lying newspaper.

But how joyfully they come to life when a foreign comrade arrives with fresh news from the outside, from the free world! And from a hiding place deep in the bowels of the cellar they take out precious souvenirs for him: Socialist or Communist brochures, red banners, labor nurses' armbands, material from the Amis de l'Enfance ouvrière—everything that they had lived for.

In the house opposite, the Nazis have installed a giant loudspeaker in order to convert their "Marxist" neighbors with blasts of Goebbels's speeches and the "Horst Wessel Song." But no one gets discouraged over such trifles: a little cotton in the ears does the trick.

Nor has good humor disappeared. As we gather around meager pieces of bread spread with margarine, the grandfather, a municipal employee, recounts while laughing how he and his colleagues have been forced to join the NSBO." Once a fortnight, these elders have to come together and drone the fascist anthems like children.

Mischievously, a small boy shouts: "Mama, do you know who burnt the Reichstag?" The prudent mother makes a sign to speak more quietly and goes to close the window. "The SASS brothers!"

The Sasses, bank robbers, are as famous in Germany as the Bonnot gang is in our country. But the "brothers" the child means are actually the SA and the SS.

It's ten o'clock in the evening. To honor the foreigner, trusted friends and neighbors have been invited to gather around the radio. Suddenly, the animated conversation dies down. The father makes a sign that the time is approaching while, feverishly turning the dial, the son tries to tune in Moscow.

You could hear a pin drop. Finally, the forbidden song comes through. Watching such a scene, one cannot despair. Who knows whether tomorrow holds in store prison, torture, or death? But this evening, as every evening, deep in countless households, lips take up the chorus and sing with low voices: " *'Tis the final conflict.*"[39]

39. The first line of the refrain of "The Internationale."

13   *Their Prisons*

n Paris, I had been given the name of a rank-and-file Socialist militant. After I arrive, I inquire if one can see him without compromising him. Is he at liberty?

A good woman offers to accompany me and mounts her bicycle. But when we ring at our friend's door, we guess right away that some misfortune has occurred. The children, left on their own, are crying in the garden. Finally, the mother, her eyes red, lets us in.

"*They* came for him yesterday . . ."

Beside her stands a neighbor, features drawn, the wife of a Communist whose husband had also fallen into *their* clutches.

No bread in the home. The prisoner has no right to unemployment relief. When he is freed, the state will claim twelve francs a day from him for detention costs and will deduct this from his future wages.

But the courageous mother doesn't want to speak of her poverty; she is thinking about her companion, perhaps tortured and beaten bloody. "You see, in Germany today it's like during the war. You're never sure of what tomorrow will bring. You live peacefully in your own home, you even surprise yourself at not being worried, and an hour later you're torn from your residence . . . for a day? a month? a year? forever?" She holds back her tears: "Nobody knows. If you are lucky, you can make it through. But if you wind up with sadists, you can come out mutilated, mad, or dead."

The neighbor, who has been listening and weeping, interrupts: "And when they come back, they can't say a word. They make them sign a paper stating they've been well treated. Take my husband, I've questioned him day and night. He'll never loosen his tongue . . . I'll never know."

Or, they answer like a young fellow we know: "Never again will I get involved in politics, never again . . ." That's all you can get out of them.

———————

A comrade who went through this hell promised to meet me and talk about it. But at the last minute, sensing the horrible danger that loomed over him, aware that he was being spied upon and followed, he let me know that he'd changed his mind. But others, so many others, do talk. And in their fixed gaze I relive the mad terror of those first months.

In the middle of Berlin, a kind of red brick tower sits atop a grassy knoll. The swastika flies over the building. "Here," a friend tells me, "we heard cries, so many cries, that *they* had to bring in an orchestra to cover them up. And even today, there still must be friends in there. But we know nothing."

Another, a fellow from Wedding, recounts with a trembling voice: "Imagine, one day I heard a noise in the street and saw a gathering . . . I went down and asked what was going on. *They* were searching the home of some Communist friends. They were demolishing everything in the apartment and beating up the family. Suddenly, I saw a guy covered in blood who couldn't stand it anymore leap over the railing and crash into the sidewalk at my feet, his legs broken."

Then there are those who have been left in a cellar in waist-deep water for several days, or who have been made to get on and off their knees five hundred times. Others have had the swastika carved into their skulls with a knife. But today, the victors prefer less visible punishments; like beating you with a truncheon on the back of the thighs and then making you run; or making you stand with arms outstretched for an hour while they fire revolver shots under your arms.

"To give you an idea of how they've refined their techniques," a friend says to me, "listen to this story. In a prison cell, they place a provocateur among a bunch of Communists. He tries to saw through the bars on the window and proposes to the others that they escape. But in the courtyard below, sa's are waiting, guns in hand. The comrades are suspicious and refuse. So the sa's burst in and cruelly whip them for having sawed through the bars."

Elsewhere, in a makeshift prison, there's a power failure: "Who cut the current?" shout the Brown jailors. Nobody is guilty, nobody answers. "Fine, we'll draw lots to see who's guilty."

A teacher offers himself up—"It's me"—and is beaten senseless.

Someone has come looking for me.

A Socialist militant. He has suffered doubly, as a Socialist and as a Jew. Since being freed, he has kept quiet and tried to rid his memory of the horrible images. But this evening, he makes an effort despite himself. With head in hands, he talks slowly, as if in a dream: "They made me mount a platform, like a trained dog. The prisoners formed the public. They made me say in a loud voice, "I am —, the biggest Jewish pig in the city." Then, for a very long time they made me walk on all fours under the table. A young SA leader, a "papa's boy," riding crop in hand, then entered the room and shouted, "Well, here's the bastard I've been wanting to beat with my own hands for such a long time!"

"And how did the prisoners react?"

"Some pretended to burst with laughter. But others were ashamed and later came to tell me from the bottom of their heart, "—, we're with you.""

He stops, hands frozen, then regains his composure: "Then, they made me go down into a cellar where there was an enormous furnace. I had to throw bundles of working-class newspapers and Marxist books into it. As I'm weak and already old, this was very hard. Some paper that had already ignited fell back onto the ground. Threatening me with a revolver, they made me sit down in the flames."

He stops. The words stick in his throat. And when I ask, "These SA's, were they adolescents? Adults? Had they been drinking?"

"They were very young . . . not at all drunk . . . but deranged . . . undoubtedly from deprivation, from an abnormal adolescence. And if I were to tell you everything!"

There are things one cannot transcribe. The human beast is capable of a thousand depraved caprices.

[In the 1945 edition:

There are things one cannot transcribe . . . I think back to this statement made by a smug petit bourgeois, overheard the day before last: "It's the first time that a country has made its revolution without shedding a drop of blood."

The Tartuffes!]

The press tells us that in Geneva, Dr. Ley has proposed a visit, at his expense, to Germany's concentration camps in response to the challenge of Léon Jouhaux, the secretary of the French CGT. I decide to take him up on the offer. I dash over to the police prefecture and state my identity: a member of the CGT, sent by the *Populaire*. In the interest of truth, I offer to visit a camp of my choosing. I merely ask for an elementary guarantee: that the answer, affirmative or negative, be given without delay so that they can't "prepare" for my visit.

And for three days, they play with me. The prefect of police is away, then without sufficient authority; the minister of the interior can't be found. Receiving no satisfaction, I get back on the train.

But if I found out how seriously to take Dr. Ley's sincerity, I also managed to see men in prison without authorization.

At Oranienburg, a long, gray wall. Then a heavy iron door. I climb onto the seat of my bicycle and grasp at the prison bars. What a bizarre spectacle! Human beings, shaggy and bearded, dressed in gray overalls, are in a courtyard under the guard of armed youths. One of them, undoubtedly a well-known militant, is forced to command: "Get up! Lie down!" They flatten themselves against the sticky mud, out of breath, in a daze . . .

When the exercise is over, they will have to sing the "Horst Wessel Song," while a comrade keeps time. For hours, they will have to shout thunderous "Heil Hitler!'s," listen to "national reeducation" lectures, and manufacture swastikas. Then, bellies empty, they'll be crammed into barrack rooms that are too small.

And there are hundreds of thousands just like them all over Germany.

In front of the police headquarters, trucks covered with canvas are waiting.[40] Suddenly, the canvas is lifted. A human cargo—young proletarians in shirt-sleeves with their bikes and motorcycles—is absorbed by the prison. Every day, thousands are arrested this way: imprison some, release others, it's a whole system of government.

A cherub-faced Steel Helmet defends the gate. The friend who accompanies me asks to speak to a prisoner.

40. In the 1945 edition, this paragraph is preceded by "Elsewhere, I would be even more successful."

"Yes, but only for a second," stammers the adolescent. As soon as he calls the person involved, hundreds of faces appear at the windows in youthful bunches.

Finally, here is the comrade. I have time to utter, "I come from France . . . How's the food? Sleeping accommodation? Morale?"

"Food: detestable; sleeping accommodation: even worse; morale: excellent!"

Already, he's gone. At the windows, signs of farewell. The fellows silently cry out their faith to us with their gazes. We've understood: *Freiheit! Rotfront!*

14 *A New Beginning*

I s Social Democracy still alive?[41] If so, in what condition? A short preamble is necessary before answering these questions. The workers' movement today *in no way* resembles what it was a few months ago. Under present conditions, can one seriously speak of parties? Can this name be given to the small groups of militants who have come forth from the ruins and operate under conditions of illegality and often with very poor contacts?

When I say "today," I naturally mean at the time of my trip, in May and the beginning of June 1933.[42] My testimony has the validity of a snapshot: it succeeds only in capturing a minute of a fugitive reality.

At first, I felt my way along.[43] Then, chance was kind to me. Strolling down the street of a large city, I suddenly spied in the window of a bookstore— lost island that it was—a book by Romain Rolland.[44]

I entered the store. On the tables, Socialist brochures; on the shelves, books by Marx and Engels. Really!

41. In the 1945 edition, this section is entitled "The End of an Illusion," and it begins with the following paragraph: "*Freiheit!* . . . Freedom! . . . This was the rallying cry, now but a quaint relic of the Socialists. I hear readers asking me, "Is Social Democracy still alive?"

42. Earlier, Guérin gives April–May 1933 as the time of this second trip; apparently, it extended at least into early June.

43. In the 1945 edition, this paragraph begins: "You can well imagine that this question haunted me from the moment of my arrival in Germany. How could I get a clear view of things? At first . . ."

44. This would be particularly subversive, since on May 14, 1933, Rolland sent a letter to the editor of the *Kölnische Zeitung* denouncing the Nazi regime.

A clerk came forward, somber and suspicious. But then he realized that he was dealing with a French comrade: "You see, if you had come tomorrow, you wouldn't have found a thing. They're going to close the bookstore, just like on the floor above where they've already shut down the newspaper. All the Marxist books will be seized and burned."

I looked at those beautiful editions for the last time, the glory of the bookstore and of German socialism: I wanted to take everything away with me, rescue it all from the executioner's wrath.

But then an old employee came out timidly from behind the shelves and, while his hand trembled, stammered out, "I've been a militant for forty years. I've been here for twenty years. We should have united against them."

The young man shakes my hand and says gloomily, "Try party headquarters. Perhaps there's still somebody there."

And in fact, in a large, empty office I find a secretary, alone, arms hanging loosely, utterly crushed: "They came this morning to seize all the party's assets. I expect to be arrested at any moment. We've gone bankrupt. We should officially dissolve the party ourselves right away and start over with a clean slate, with other men."[45]

Perhaps, but this militant's opinion didn't prevail (he was arrested the next day). The central leadership equivocated for a long time. Instead of courageously throwing itself into illegal action, the party tried to come to terms with the adversary. And for weeks on end, the rank-and-file comrades were kept waiting, demoralized, inactive, and finally indignant.

"The May 17 vote of the parliamentary caucus ratifying the regime[46] is the coup de grace," a boy with energetic features, a former section head

45. On May 10, 1933, a day of book burnings throughout Germany, "an order was issued for the confiscation of all the property of the Social Democratic Party and of its newspapers, as well as of the Reichsbanner and its Press" (*BT,* 153). Property of the Communist party and its press had already been confiscated several months earlier, although a formal order legalizing this was issued on May 27, 1933. The Social Democrats were excluded from all parliaments following decrees issued on June 23 and July 7, 1933.

46. On May 17, 1933, the Socialists gave their support to Hitler's declaration on foreign policy delivered before the Reichstag. On the same day, a decree prohibited strikes throughout Germany. The *BT* notes that even the SPD's support for Hitler's declaration and their repudiation of the section of the Social Democratic party executive which had emigrated "proved to have been in vain." The efforts made by Löbe, the new party leader, "to secure toleration from the Hitler government" failed (*BT,* 155).

of the Reichsbanner, admitted to me. "Now, between us and them, it's over . . . over forever."

He said this with a broken voice, like someone who for a long time and in spite of everything had wanted to remain confident, hopeful, and patient: "We've had more than our fill. If you only knew! I'll never forget the night of March 5,[47] when we got on our motorcycles in all the big cities of Germany and converged on Berlin begging for combat orders."

"And what did they reply?"

"Keep calm! And above all don't shed any blood!"

For a group of human beings to deserve to be called a "party" in a country as disciplined and hierarchical as Germany, the minimum requirements are that the members pay their dues, meet—secretly or not—and receive instructions from their leaders.

"We don't pay anymore. We don't meet anymore. The leaders either stay at home bowing their heads before the storm, are in prison, or have fled," a Socialist warden at a youth hostel explains to me. And he adds, "Besides, it's almost better that the 'elders' get out of the way. They no longer have anyone's confidence. Only the young will be able to do something."

"And you?"

He sighs: "I have two children to feed. The Nazis have said to me, "If you want to stay at the hostel, join our party." I told them that you can't change the heart of a Socialist just like that. But my wife insisted—Alas!, on top of everything, we have to fight against our wives!—and I had to give in."[48]

In Lübeck, another militant explains his confusion to me: "I tell you, I don't know where I am anymore. We've been abandoned by our lead-

---

47. The night of March 5–6, 1933, as the 1945 edition specifies. This would have been in response to the elections of March 5, in which the Nazis elected 288 deputies to the Reichstag—not a majority. On March 21, the Communist deputies were forbidden to take their seats, and on March 24, with support from the Zentrum, the Ermächtigungsgesetz (Enabling Act) was adopted, empowering the government to proclaim and enforce laws without the approval of the Reichstag, thus providing the "legal" basis for Hitler's dictatorship. The SPD caucus alone opposed the Enabling Act.

48. See note 22 of the Introduction for excerpts from letters of resignation to the SPD motivated by similar concerns.

ers . . . without newspapers . . . without slogans . . . and what's worst of
all is that good comrades—especially members of the Reichsbanner—who
could have brought some clarity to the situation believe they have done the
right thing by joining the Steel Helmets by the hundreds under the pretext
of provoking discord between the reactionaries and the Nazis and to pro-
cure weapons. Perhaps they were right, but I think they've only made
matters worse! Today, you don't know where your friends are and where the
enemy is."

On the table I spot, not without surprise, an issue of the *Volksbote,* the
former Socialist newspaper of the city.

"What's this? Is it appearing again?"

"Yes, but under Nazi control! And, for editor in chief . . . a well-known
Socialist militant from Lübeck! You see the trap! Workers can still believe
that they're reading their old paper . . .

And he hands the paper to me. I read, stunned: "Of course, the vast
majority of former Socialists are taking a wait-and-see attitude today, but
they display no hostility whatsoever to the new regime. Comrades are
thinking that if the new men do better than the old ones, this will already
be something. All we ask is that our distress be relieved. If the Nazis do
something for the workers, then we will cooperate with them, despite all
the hatred and bitterness of the past. . . . The task of the new *Lübecker
Volksbote* is to seal this alliance between the government and the people."
Signed, Max Ahrenholdt, editor in chief.

"Naturally, this 'militant' is a traitor!"

"Some say so. Others think it's good for us to keep some of our men at
our old newspaper. But where is the truth? Yesterday, we were brothers in
struggle, today you don't even know whose hand you can shake!"

And, discouraged, he throws up his hands.

———

As often happens in life, here the best and the worst go together. On the
one hand, there's the enormous disaster, the cowardice, the desertions, the
suicides. On the other, the unswerving loyalty, the youth, the faith. Let's
seek out those who carry the future in them.

In August 1932, at a Franco-German workers children's camp at Draveil,
I knew a young aide of the Amis de l'Enfance ouvrière. The unemployment
bureau had cut off his benefits and sent him to work as cheap labor in the

country, where he became a farmboy for some greedy, tough peasants. Rabid Hitlerites, they were suspicious and spied on him.

I find him in bed in his tiny room: he injured himself while working and has a fever. As I abruptly open the door, he rubs his eyes to make sure he isn't dreaming.

"You!"

And then he explains: "I'm here for a year! They told me it's prison or the contract. So, I signed. I'm all alone, without a friend or a book. They confiscated my pamphlets. Around me, nobody but narrow-minded people full of hatred."

He looks me in the eyes: "But I'm as you knew me." He speaks to me of the French workers' movement as if it were his own; and when it comes time to take leave of the only friend he would see in twelve months, he murmurs: "I'm not complaining . . . I'm eighteen years old, with my life ahead of me. I will see the triumph of socialism."

A gray-haired man, an old freethinking proletarian militant, maintains the same certainty in the twilight of his existence: "Perhaps I won't see it personally. But you will. Our generation failed at its task. You see, I believe in the crystallization of an *absolutely new* movement, which will come forth from the depth of our working class . . . *a new beginning* . . ."

He puts sugar in his coffee, smiles, and gazes at me with blue eyes of limpid purity: "For, deep among the masses, in this youth that hasn't yet had its word, there are marvelous reserves, virgin lands!"

And already in Berlin, Leipzig, and other cities all over Germany, groups of those under thirty are springing up, making a complete break with the old ideologies and leaders. The saj* (Young Socialist Workers) are the right yeast for the dough. The groups are slowly bringing together comrades driven by the need to act, distributing clandestine newspapers, seeking liaison with other revolutionary nuclei, with no concern for political tendencies.

About ten youths sit around a table in the lamplight. There are boys present who were timorous and meek last year. Today, they proclaim joyfully that they have been transfigured.

Of course, there is still some hesitation among them. They have everything to learn about illegal struggle; some of them continue to distrust the

Communists. There are those who feel that before acting they should take a detour and go back to the theoretical sources of Marxism.

But they all want to fight, and all agree: "We believed too deeply in the virtues of bourgeois democracy. On May 17, that illusion was swept away for good. Now, we know no other watchwords than those of Marx and Lenin."[49]

49. The 1945 edition reads: "On May 17, the *democratic* illusion was swept away for good. Now we know no other watchwords than those of Marx and Lenin: dictatorship of the proletariat!"

15   *Underground*

Would you like to see the revolutionary proletariat with your own eyes?" a comrade in Hamburg proposes.[50]

It's five o'clock in the afternoon. We head toward the port, still lively despite the ravages of the Depression. And suddenly, he invites me to descend an imposing stairway.

"Are we taking an underground train?"

"No, we're just going to visit the tunnel under the Elbe."

Once we're down there, it's impossible to move forward. An obscure mass flows toward us from the somber vaults. And then, suddenly, our eyes are confronted with a spectacle worthy of the film *Metropolis*:[51] five enormous elevators are ferrying the throng of workers nonstop back up toward the light. A lone Schupo is sufficient to direct the crowd toward this or that apparatus. In orderly fashion, the men pile in. An automatic door closes behind them like a guillotine. From afar, they look like a herd in a slaughterhouse.

"Those are the fellows from the naval shipyards coming off the job."

I watch them. Hell, they don't look like sheep! Young, energetic faces. In their buttonholes, on their caps, you search in vain for a swastika. Kids in shorts and shoulder straps begging for some "national" charity harass them with their collection boxes. No one pays attention. But a little girl manages to slide a small paper flag into the hand of one of the men. Calmly—and with a gesture of controlled anger—he throws the emblem away.

Accompany me through the old streets of Hamburg and Altona with

50. In the 1945 edition, this section is entitled "Rot Front!"
51. German filmmaker Fritz Lang's vision of life in the depersonalized, machine-dominated modern city.

their worm-eaten wooden houses. You'd think you were back in the Middle Ages. But suddenly, on the sidewalk, in large, freshly traced white letters: "*Communism lives!*"

And if you venture into the foul-smelling dead-end streets, there, under the dark archways, you can read inscriptions like "Death to Hitler!" and "Long Live the Revolution!" on every wall.

In the courtyards of these slums, exhausted workers stop smoking their pipes long enough to throw us a ferocious glance: "Even today," my guide explains to me, "the police don't dare venture into this cutthroat place. They know that here there are only recalcitrants who know how to defend themselves!"[52]

As we thought, the Brown terror hasn't killed the idea of revolution. But can we say that a revolutionary party, centralized and organized from the base up, functions in Germany today? That's what I spent five weeks trying to find out.

"At first," a comrade admits, "we went through a horrible period of depression. Leaders and numerous militants were jailed and tortured . . . the havoc wreaked by informers, distributions of weapons and leaflets foiled . . ."

"And unfortunately, many defections to the other camp."

The comrade sighs: "Yes, all those 'radicalized' elements with no class consciousness, that *Lumpenproletariat*[53] that we dragged behind us like a ball and chain. Debris from the Red Front fighters, guys who liked a uniform and a scuffle and who had only one ideal: to be at the top of the heap on their own turf. These 'neighborhood terrors' went over to the adversary at the decisive moment. To make a good impression or to deaden their remorse, they became the cruelest of all. They turned over the names of their cell members and turned against their former comrades."

"But I believe that in the sa there are also many Communists who have remained loyal?"

52. Author's note: Since I wrote this, Hitler's regime has razed the old neighborhoods of Hamburg for its own security. (The note for the 1945 edition, however, reads: "Soon afterward, this neighborhood was razed by the Nazis, before the Second World War transformed the entire city of Hamburg into a pile of rubble.")

53. Note in the 1945 edition: "The expression by which Marx designated the dregs of the populace of the large cities."

"Of course. There are those for whom the Storm Troopers was the only way out, and they've resigned themselves to joining in order to avoid torture or death. And there are those whom the Nazis believe they've converted, but who wear the brown shirt because they've been threatened and forced to do so. Finally, there are the volunteers whom we've sent in ourselves. They could be shot at any moment, but they're doing fantastic work from the *inside!*"

Others confirmed this comrade's explanations. All in all, the terror has been responsible for a salutary sorting out. The dubious elements have deserted; the lukewarm and the timid have disappeared; only the best are left. You have to have seen with your own eyes with what quiet courage, what composure, what confidence in the future these well-tempered men continue the struggle.

At a street corner, two comrades take leave of me with a peaceful smile; you would think they were studious and quiet youths. One's father is a Steel Helmet, the other's a pastor; they want to give their blood for a proletarian Germany: "See you tomorrow!"

The next day, I waited in vain. During a nocturnal meeting, they were arrested. Will they ever be seen again? But others have already taken their place.

———

After the crushing blow, the movement is slowly reborn.

You have to start over from the beginning: first of all, you must grope around in the night, trying to find the survivors from your cell and then seeking out liaisons with other cells. *Liaisons!* It's a question of life or death, and today the word is on everyone's lips. In some cities and districts, it has taken only a few weeks for life to surge forth from the ruins. In others, on the contrary, the devastation is such, with arrested and vanished militants, that they are only beginning to feel their way. At times progress has been rapid, but a sudden accident such as new arrests can compromise these patient efforts for weeks.

Deprived of leaders or having only rare contacts with them, these small groups have learned to fend for themselves, taking initiatives and improvising under conditions of illegality. For proletarians once pressed into activity like cogs in a machine, this has been a fruitful test of their sound common sense.

Here is a mother with five young children to take care of. She is one of the rare survivors—the rallying point of her cell. Each week, a comrade brings her a bundle of illegal leaflets. She passes some along to a few friends with whom she is in contact.

"And the rest?"

"The rest? I distribute them . . . in mailboxes.[54] Naturally, I choose those who might get something out of reading them."

While with simplicity and modesty she explains her perilous work to me, the imprudent child at the window shouts what he learned when he was born: "Rotfront!"

What ingenuity these novices must deploy! The clandestine publications, run off deep in cellars, circulated in abundance: *Truth, Workers' Voice, Unity,* and so on. Those who don't have duplicating machines send their wives to buy children's printing sets at the toy counters of the big stores, then use the movable rubber characters to compose small leaflets.[55]

"How do we do it?" A comrade who has become a real specialist in the matter explains. "Look, for example, we print a prospectus of several pages with an innocent title on the cover, let's say the Salvation Army. We distribute it at the factory gates or even in the barracks of the Reichswehr. You have to open it to find our prose! From the rooftop bars of the department stores, we shower leaflets onto the street below. If it's done skillfully, it's impossible to find the guilty party. In a café, we ask for the newspaper and between two articles, with a 'line' taken out of our pocket and a damp pad, we inscribe a judicious sentence."

He takes some tiny paper rectangles out of his wallet. I read: "*Torchlight parades don't bring bread. Spread the word.*" Or, "*Hitler's first act: to betray his program, to annul not a single decree; to send socialism packing with Papen. Spread the word.*"

"We paste these up on shop fronts, in the subway. . . . Then there are the pictures on cigarette packages: we print a sentence on the back, and our kids redistribute these pictures to other kids in the public squares. In this way, many parents wind up reading them . . . and I haven't even

54. In the 1945 edition, Guérin explains in a note to his French audience how this would be possible: "In Germany, there are no concierges, and each tenant has his own mailbox."

55. For a detailed contemporary account of resistance publications, as reported by the Nazi press itself, see *BT* (333–40).

spoken about the newspaper boys who slip a *Rote Fahne* into copies of the *Völkischer Beobachter!*"

Of course, most of these tricks are foiled quickly enough; but they come up with others even more quickly. The comrade takes me by the arm and says with the gaiety of a schoolboy: "Listen to this. The height of refinement is to distribute leaflets to the SA that are written in the fascist style. That way, they read us! Our old Marxist phrases don't carry any weight today, but there are a thousand ways of upsetting them *from the inside,* and sowing discord among them."

And here's the bouquet: "A little while ago, our leaflets were having such an effect that things degenerated into an incredible brawl, with guys at each other's throats accusing each other of writing and distributing them!"

16   *Toward Unity in Action?*

One fine Saturday in May, small groups of scantily dressed young Berliners, arms and legs tanned by the sun, set out on their bicycles, a full complement of camping supplies in their heavy rucksacks. Their meeting place: an isolated pine grove on the shore of a lake. But they aren't getting together simply to partake in the joys of swimming or to lounge about on the warm sand. Every one of them represents a district of the Young Communists from the capital. And far from the gaze of inquisitive eyes, they're going to hold a kind of meeting—as long as the police don't come and seize their bikes and motorcycles in a dragnet operation.

Among the Reds, as with the Socialists, the youth are the most active. Less familiar to their adversaries than their elders, less watched by informers, they have more successfully weathered the storm. But has the catastrophe opened their eyes? Will they, like the young Socialists, reject the slogans that led to defeat?

Of course, some of them are quite lucid. But this brother and sister, at once so fanatical and so kind, repeat to me in a calm tone of voice, like children reciting their catechism: "Our line was entirely correct." It's impossible to get anything else out of them.

"*Our line was entirely correct.*" That was the theme of Heckert's report to the executive of the Communist International in April; and it's still the tune of the apparatus.[56] For a clandestine apparatus does exist within the party. It has better contacts with Moscow than with the small dispersed groups at the base. And so, a little like a deaf person, it gives orders but can't

56. See note 12 of the Introduction for an excerpt from the Comintern's resolution.

■   *153*

hear any response. It is not afraid to affirm that the fascist dictatorship *opens the way to proletarian revolution*—true, perhaps, over the long term but ridiculous in the present context. It advocates public and even armed demonstrations in the streets and workplaces. It continues to send tendentious and exaggerated reports to the external press and to the International, when true revolutionaries should measure the *exact* relationship of forces.

But how do the rank-and-file comrades feel, those who have managed to reconstitute their cells on their own? What do they say?

Of course, there are still the blind, like the one who thanks fascism from the bottom of his heart for having given the coup de grace to Social Democracy, or another who winds up admitting to me with disarming candor, "I like Hitler a hundred times better than Severing" [the former Prussian Social Democratic minister].

But among the majority, a profound change has taken place. That comrade from Wedding, my friend from last year, used to have the faith of a monk. Now I find him thinner, pale, with a ferocious expression: "We screwed ourselves but good! Ah, to think we gave up that neighborhood without a fight!"

For this comrade, the Köslinerstrasse, the famous Red street of "Red" Wedding, was still the fortress of the proletariat, the center of the world. To see the swastika flying there broke his heart.

"And what illusions we concocted for ourselves with the ballot! Now, I say, 'Worker, fend for yourself; don't go begging orders from the leaders anymore'; that's all over! They'll never get us to do that again."

In vain, I try to point out that if their confidence in the leadership was exaggerated, the opposite excess would be dangerous. He sticks to his guns: "To hell with the intellectuals! They should let us do our job. After all, we're the ones they beat and bloody."

An artist, an old Bolshevik who's been celebrated in the USSR, spoke to me in even more violent language. When he speaks today, his hands tremble with anger and pain: "They're busy with their Five-Year Plan; well and good! But in God's name, don't let them mix in here anymore and teach us about fighting. It's for us, and us alone, do you understand, to struggle against Hitler. We're in the thick of the fight. We'll know better than they, thousands of kilometers away, what has to be done. *We* see things as they are!"

I can't believe my ears. The following diatribe is etched in my memory, even if I have no way of verifying it: "If you only knew what's been going on! Really, our comrades in the USSR are disheartening! A Communist fugitive takes refuge on a Soviet ship in a northern German port. Mercilessly, they reject him. If he's still alive today, he's in the hands of the Brown bandits. Another, a Hungarian, is expelled from Germany on twenty-four hours' notice; he begs the Russian embassy to issue him a visa. He is refused."

And what's more, while the whole world is boycotting Hitler, they are renewing the Berlin treaty! In January, 60 percent of German exports went to Russia, and now they're getting ready to place new orders!

Other militants no longer hesitate to say out loud what they were thinking to themselves last year: Why this strange policy of the *front unique?* Why was an armistice with the Socialists only signed at the beginning of March, when it was too late, after having been rejected in June 1932? And why the wretched trade union tactics that deprived revolutionaries of any influence over workers on the job? And what about that absurd, anti-Marxist slogan "national liberation" that played right into the hands of fascism?

A comrade insists on this last point and considers it essential: "If you want to understand Hitler's triumph, you should never forget that for a Marxist the main enemy is in his own country. First of all you have to fight your own capitalists. But we Germans, Communists included, have blamed all our misfortunes on the *Diktat,*[57] even on the Depression. We considered foreign capital to be our main enemy."

While we talk in hushed voices in the street or, like conspirators, seek refuge in the back room of a café, I try to take stock. I admire the frankness and courage with which these comrades, always eager to correct and improve themselves, make their mea culpa. But has the "apparatus" been through the same agony? My friends seem to me like the young traveler who leaves his parents' home for the first time to discover the outside

57. Note from the 1945 edition: "The Treaty of Versailles."

world. When he returns to the paternal hearth, he's stunned at the realization that he and his family no longer speak the same language.

Already, small oppositional groups are springing up within the party, publishing tracts and trying to make their new ideas prevail without useless polemics.

A friend who belongs to one of these groups bitterly confides, "You have no idea what a disastrous impression I get when I read Heckert's report or the printed *Rote Fahne* [for there are also duplicated *Rote Fahne*s that circulate but aren't put out by the apparatus]. The same old rigid, stereotypical words that are no longer worth a thing in action."

"But when contacts improve, will you be able to impose your perspective on the apparatus? Who will be stronger, it or you?"

Uncertain, he shakes his head. "That's the whole problem."

Has the catastrophe at least served to hasten the unification of working-class forces? Since last summer, there has been constant progress in the two parties toward common action, and this in spite of the leadership. Will this trend finally triumph?

Driven by a sincere concern for unity, Communists are multiplying their contacts with Socialist workers. Small nocturnal meetings are held secretly in the homes of one or the other where, without uselessly dwelling on past errors, they envisage a common future.

As well as Socialists and Communists, other groups continue their efforts: militants of the Socialist Workers' party (SAP),* Brandlerists (Communist opposition), and, last, the Bolshevik-Leninists, or Trotskyists; their clandestine newspapers, intelligently edited and rich in information, are among the best. If their disciples form only a tiny nucleus, it nevertheless seems that Trotsky's personal influence is growing. "*The only one who could see clearly,*" comrades who only yesterday treated him as a renegade are beginning to say.[58]

58. Heiden summarizes: "Trotzky demanded that the Communists create a united front through a pact with the Social Democrats, while the Communists under Stalin's leadership clung to the view that the Social Democrats must be smashed before fascism could effectively be combated, and for that reason fascism must come to power" (461). Trotsky himself had been stripped of all offices, then expelled from the party and Soviet Russia. He wrote about the dangers of Nazism from exile. In 1940, he was murdered at his home in Mexico by a Stalinist agent.

But isn't this dissipation of good intentions into a fine spray of tiny sects dangerous? Doesn't each have the tendency to ignore the others, to believe that it holds the absolute truth? "Undoubtedly," an ardent unifier explains to me, "but deep down everyone agrees, everyone wants to see the unification of working-class forces into a single revolutionary party in order to defeat fascism. Only, to get there, there are two possible paths: some believe that the Communist party can still be put back on course and become the rallying point of the German proletariat. Others who are discouraged not by the heroism of its militants but by the Russian tactics want to found a new revolutionary party."

"And your prognosis?"

He sighs, hesitating: "Everything depends on Moscow!"

———

On May 11, the entire working class of Breslau—Socialists, Communists, SAP—had already come together over the coffin of comrade Eckstein, victim of the executioners. The swell of workers, a witness tells me, was so dense and their anger so strong that the Brownshirts deserted the streets. "Rotfront's" reverberated from the heart of the cemetery. And since then, there's been a continuous procession past the modest tomb.

Perhaps for unity in action to be sealed, martyrs were and will continue to be necessary . . .

17   *And Now?*

f you have read Alphonse Daudet,* you know that sometimes two men live inside a single being. When the poor Tartarin can't reconcile his opposites, he lets Don Quixote and Sancho Panza dialogue freely inside him. A similar misadventure has befallen me at the end of my journey. The conductor who punches my ticket on the train home sees only one traveler; but we are two.

The Optimist: "My dear Pessimist, go have a cigarette in the corridor so that we can each explain our position. You look grieved, my friend. Shall I confess to you that I return from that accursed country much more lighthearted?"

The Pessimist: "At least *try* to justify yourself!"

The Optimist: "I fully intend to. In the first place, I have a feeling that these gentlemen are not as strong as they appear. They have won too easily, too quickly. It's true that they've destroyed all the parties. But there remains one which nobody ever talks about, either there or outside, and yet which is devilishly important: the army! Do you believe that the fascist gangrene has so thoroughly penetrated that "state within a state"? Have you noticed how its chiefs are careful to remain in the background, far from the melee? For my part, I was able to talk with some of the young soldiers, and I didn't find them all that contaminated. Just how far will they let Hitler go and for how long? And as for that old weasel Schleicher in forced retirement at Postsdam, don't you think he's biding his time?[59]

"You shrug your shoulders. But tell me, does this dog's breakfast of a party with its millions of new members inspire confidence in you? Of

59. Schleicher was slain on June 30, 1934.

course, they've managed to filter the recruits by imposing a probationary period on them. But look how many they've accepted and even enlisted against their will. Naturally, they flatter themselves by believing that they've converted or "reeducated" all those people. But the opposite may happen. Perhaps the sa and the ss, those infamous pillars of the regime, are actually worm-eaten. There are all kinds in there, now; reactionaries, Marxists, Apaches, and National Bolsheviks; a fine mix indeed! It's true that there are purges and that some are sent to concentration camps, but this, it seems to me, is in fact a sign of disarray! Don't forget that the adversary slipped away without ever putting up a fight. That was its weakness, perhaps today that is its strength. Marxism is being reborn, like a hydra with a thousand heads, among the Brownshirts themselves. It's fighting from behind a mask, which is a great advantage right now. How long will they continue to feed these starving youths and keep them in line? There's something else we don't know!

"You see, the main Nazi leaders could soon be outflanked. The masses are becoming more and more demanding. There's talk of mutiny, and Hitler himself is forced to get angry and remove his mask: '*There will be no new revolution!*' And that's how he thinks he's going to calm his troops! For my part, I won't be surprised if the current picks up speed; perhaps then other men, like Gregor Strasser, for example, will resurface.[60] And even though our comrades are hardly ready to rise to the opportunity, we'll see ordinary people trade the *Brown* for the *Red* even more rapidly than they had abandoned the *Red* for the *Brown!*

"And then, fascism is entangled in a web of inextricable contradictions. It finds it impossible to accomplish its anticapitalist program . . . or even its anti-Semitic one. See how tactfully it deals with the department stores and the big Jewish shareholders![61] It has taken care not to touch big industrial and commercial capital. Isn't the naming of Hugenberg's successor in the Ministry of the Economy symbolic? This Mr. Kurt Schmitt is the man of the big insurance companies!

"You say the petite bourgeoisie will support Hitler to the very end? Yes, but only if he throttles their competitors, the big sharks, and domesticates

---

60. Gregor Strasser was also murdered on June 30, 1934.
61. See the Introduction for a further discussion of Nazi attitudes toward the "Jewish" department stores and, in many cases, their non-Jewish creditors.

high finance. And in the final analysis, only if business picks up. That adds up to a lot of conditions!

"Obviously, there's the infamous 'internal colonization.' Hugenberg has been replaced in Agriculture by an ardent partisan of land redistribution. Moreover, for reasons of foreign policy, they're determined to reinforce the populations of the frontier provinces. They'll do something, that's for sure. But will they dare to sacrifice enough feudal landowners to satisfy the peasant masses in the east? I doubt it!

"Despite their fraudulent statistics, unemployment hasn't improved one iota. They've only given work to some by taking it away from others. How will they keep their promises? How will they manage to occupy eight million people without work over the next four years? How will they avoid inflation?

"By carving out territories for themselves in the east at the expense of the USSR? That's the old idea of Alfred Rosenberg and other "White Russians" who, at the beginning, served as the godparents of National Socialism. In theory, it's very tempting. But in practice, it's another story! In the meantime, economic relations with the Soviets remain excellent!"

The Pessimist: "I've listened to you, my friend, without interrupting. But more than once you must have noticed a smile at the corners of my mouth. Not that your arguments are absurd. Of course the Third Reich finds itself confronted with serious difficulties. But do you believe that Italy and the USSR haven't known economic contradictions over the past ten years? The two regimes are still standing. Don't forget that National Socialism is the synthesis, the end product, the fruit of two experiments. Hitler, who is not an imbecile, has learned the art of governing from Stalin and Mussolini. And he's been preparing for a long time. With its ministries and services, his party has been a veritable Reich within the Reich for several years already. Haven't you noticed with what skill he settled into place between the end of January and late February? Nothing was left to chance. In organizational terms, no one has ever done better; our comrades were literally taken unaware.

"And then, don't ever forget that Germany is an essentially bureaucratic country. Once one has conquered that immense mass of functionaries, police, and soldiers, one is their master for a long time. Granted, they still have to find work for a lot of their supporters, but they will fix them up. And those they dismiss will remain in their clutches: in labor camps and state work sites. They're busy creating a fearsome secret police. The further they go with that, the riskier and more perilous illegal work will become. Through a cycle of arrests, releases, and terror, they will succeed in sidelining many militants from the struggle . . .

"You say that the masses want 'socialism'? But they don't all want the same socialism. That of the petit bourgeois isn't at all that of the peasant or the worker. They'll play upon these differences and find a bone for each group to gnaw on. In the meantime, Hitler is a new Napoleon for the small landowning peasantry. If the mutinies continue, they will be merciless. If they have to get their troops back in line or reestablish control over a critical situation, they'll take whatever extreme measures are necessary.

"Marxism, a hydra with a thousand heads? Go see for yourself! In the streets of Altona,[62] the kids of the Red proletarians bawl out the "Horst Wessel Song" as they leave school! They'll get the children while they're in the cradle, they'll fashion the new generations![63]

"Inflation? New economic opportunities? They can manage these for quite a while with their autarchy, their monopoly over foreign exchange, their fictional currency. You've already seen how casually they repudiated half of their foreign debt! If they need money, they'll draw from the bank tills, like Mussolini. It's fine for a liberal economist to ooh and ah! Believe me, they haven't run out of tricks yet! And then, you very carefully avoided broaching the essential question—the upturn in business. Perhaps you are not aware that in America the situation is improving? Of course, capitalism can only survive with the hideous chancre of unemployment. But if it becomes possible to find work for even two or three million of the people now unemployed in Germany, what a godsend for Hitler!"

---

62. Near Hamburg, this working-class center and Communist party stronghold was the site of "Bloody Sunday" on July 17, 1932. After the Papen government lifted the ban on the SA and SS, the two Nazi groups announced their intention to stage a propaganda march in Altona, and the "request" was approved by the local SPD police president. Seven thousand Nazis were met with KPD opposition; the police intervened, and eighteen people were killed, most by the police. After the Nazis seized power, fifteen arrested Communists were tried for murder; four were executed and the others were jailed.

63. The indoctrination of children, especially those who have no memory of life before the Nazi seizure of power, is discussed in Erika Mann's impassioned book *School for Barbarians* (1939).

At the conclusion of this investigation and this voyage, I will speak only about that of which I'm certain.[64]

I saw the Brown plague pass there. I have seen what it has done to a great civilized country. My testimony is devoid of any chauvinism. You have not heard me say, as is murmured within our own Socialist ranks here in France, "It's all come to pass because they're Boches!"

Nor will I say, like the Social Democratic leader Wels, that the German working class *demonstrated that it wasn't up to the task.* If its leadership betrayed it, it isn't the will to struggle that was lacking, or that is lacking today.

I saw fascism with my own eyes. Today, I know what it is. And I feel that we need to examine our own consciences before it's too late. For ten years, we haven't given the phenomenon sufficient attention. A carnival Caesar, joked Paul-Boncour.* No, fascism isn't a masquerade.[65] Fascism is a system, an ideology, an outcome. Granted, it doesn't resolve anything, but it endures. It's the bourgeoisie's answer to the default of the working class. Without too greatly compromising the privileges of the bourgeoisie, it's an attempt to find a way out of the chaos and to establish a new form of economic planning, an ersatz socialism.

In Germany, I learned that in order to defeat fascism, you have to oppose it with a living example, a flesh-and-blood ideal. Ah, if only the USSR, by once again becoming a republic of *Soviets,* could be the irresistible pole of attraction it was after 1917!

I learned that if the working class continues to default, fascism will become generalized throughout the world. Will you wait for the blows of the truncheon to fall here? Fascism is essentially aggressive. If we let it go forward, if we remain on the defensive, it will annihilate us. It makes use of a new demagogic and revolutionary language. If we harken back to the same hackneyed clichés without breathing new life into them through our acts, if we don't strike at the heart of its formidable doctrines, if we don't learn how to respond to it, we will meet the same fate as the Italians and the

64. In the 1945 edition, this sentence is preceded by "Enough! There are perhaps better ways to spend our time than pursuing this discussion, than playing the prophet."
65. In the 1945 edition: " 'Fascism,' said the venerable Clara Zetkin as early as 1923, 'is the punishment visited upon the proletariat for not pursuing the revolution begun in Russia.' A carnival Caesar, joked another. No, fascism isn't a grotesque improvisation. Fascism is a system."

Germans. Finally, fascism is essentially a youth movement. If we don't know how to attract youth and satisfy their need for action and ideals, they may well escape and even turn against us. And if we don't purge our actions of the slightest vestiges of nationalism, we will lay the groundwork for a *national socialism.* Who knows, perhaps this groundwork is already being laid in our country . . . [66]

In the Friedrichsfeld cemetery in Berlin, there is a plain brick wall. Surrounded by the sailors and revolutionaries of 1919, Karl Liebknecht and Rosa Luxemburg sleep their final sleep. Barriers covered with barbed wire block the entrance to the humble enclosure with the order "*Do not enter!*"

This is the only corner of Germany that still belongs to us. Wilted flowers. A woman observes me with malevolent curiosity. In the distance, the Brownshirts are exercising and shouting the ritualistic triple cry: "Heil! Heil! Heil!"

Everything becomes clear. The assassinations of Karl and Rosa, the arson of the Reichstag, such is the treachery to which a bourgeoisie with its back against the wall resorts in order to prolong its rule. Not simply the *German* bourgeoisie, but the bourgeoisie plain and simple. It's no mere chance that today the fine flower of French "intellectuals" are swooning before the "strong man" from beyond the Rhine.

But to their triple cry, we respond with our own: "Workers of the world, unite!"[67]

66. In the 1945 edition, this last sentence is omitted. Instead, the following paragraph appears: "At the present time—and this is the lesson of the German experience—there are only two alternatives left: whoever is not for the revolution prepares the way—consciously or not—for fascism."

67. The 1945 editions reads: "It's no mere chance that today the fine flower of our 'gentlemen' are swooning before Hitler and Göring. As for ourselves, to their 'Heil' we respond: 'Workers of the world, unite!' "

"Ring" Youth Gangs
by Christine Fournier
(from *Die neue Weltbühne,*
January 20, 1931

Aghost that can be neither grasped nor unmasked lurks in the background of almost every trial in Berlin involving adolescents: The ghost of the wild gangs.[1] Let me remind you of the *röntgentaler* murder trial, held in Potsdam on December 6, 1928, where a group of youths from Neukölln,[2] all members of the Tarterenblut[3] gang, faced charges for deadly assault, numerous car thefts, disturbances of the peace, and arson—a veil of mystery still shrouds this case.

Wild gangs? What are they? How long have they existed? Where and how do they live? Are they comparable to the Parisian Apaches (Indians) or the Viennese Plattenbrüder (a kind of brotherhood)? In some respects, this comparison is certainly valid: in their way of life, their goals, their hatred of society. But these German gangs differ radically in structure from the other famous and notorious criminal gangs because they recruit their members predominantly among fourteen- to eighteen-year-olds. These wild gangs are organizations of neglected teenagers, juvenile "dissocials." *Dissozial,* a psychological term, means the inability to integrate oneself into society, or the unwillingness to do so, and therefore these wild gangs can be called *gemeinschafts-unguhige,* a community of those incapable of living in the community.

The history of these gangs goes far back to the time when the first Luna Parks, similar to those which still exist, were founded, back to the youth

---

1. "Ring" in the title refers to the districts of Berlin outside the city center that were linked by a circular "ring" of avenues.

2. A poor district of Berlin.

3. Blood of the Tartars.

and Roamer (hiking) movements that existed before the Great War.[4] These movements aspired toward a better future, for which their adherents were willing to work. Inversely, the gangs, whether deliberately or not, mainly thought about destroying what existed. Later, but still before the outbreak of the war, the Red Roamers was founded as a left-wing organization of proletarian teenagers who distanced themselves from criminal activities. The Red Roamers dissolved during the war, and only in 1923 was a second attempt made by the Communist youth to reform the wild gangs, to save them from an asocial life and integrate them politically. But this was only temporarily successful. The gangs had reappeared in 1916–17 during the Great Famine and as housing became an increasing problem. Back then, one could meet small groups of teenagers, most of them drunk and dressed in bright colors, who noisily roamed the streets of the outlying districts[5] of the big cities. People called them *Wanderflegel* (a *flegel* is a person who behaves in a rude way). These were predominantly young people whose fathers served in the war and whose mothers worked in factories, with nobody else caring for them. This was the beginning of today's wild gangs, whose journey into criminality we largely owe to the chaos of the peacetime inflation that followed the war, the continuing existence of unemployment, and the lack of housing.

These gangs commit a variety of crimes in the outlying districts of Berlin, such as street robbery, breaking and entering, etc. Due to their exemplary form of organization and numerous secret hiding places, the police manage to catch only individual members once in a while but never the whole group. If the police arrest a gang member, he has to stand trial. Then he serves a prison sentence or is sent to a correctional institute for juveniles. Most of the inmates of the latter institutions belong to one or another of the wild gangs. The inmate escapes, gets caught, is incarcerated again, and escapes again. I will refer to this absurdity again later. Much to their credit, some social workers have devoted their energies to these gangs and have even succeeded in establishing contact, gathering experience, and forming some general ideas about them. As examples one can cite articles

---

4. A celebratory American account of the history of the "legitimate" German youth movement, prepared in anticipation of the World Youth Peace Congress to be held in Holland in August 1928, is Ellis Chadbourne's *Youth's Crusade.*

5. The German word is *Vorstadt,* which is not a suburb in the modern sense of the term. Rather, it is a working-class district outside the heart of the city, akin to the French *faubourg.*

such as "Gangs of Neglected Teenagers as a Social and Educational Problem," by Otto Voss and Herbert Schönis, and "Cliques and Neglected Youth," by Justus Ehrhardt.[6] These social workers estimate that in all of Germany approximately fourteen thousand youths belong to the wild gangs. Among them a third are between fourteen and sixteen years old, and two-thirds are between sixteen and eighteen. It is assumed that six hundred gangs exist in Berlin alone. Social workers distinguish between hiking clubs and criminal gangs. Probably 10 percent of them deserve to be qualified as criminal; 20 percent exist on the edge of legality; 70 percent are purely hiking clubs. Among the latter, 5 percent are affiliated with the Right and 15 percent with the Left, while the rest show no interest in politics. The hiking clubs are relatively harmless. They usually dissolve at the beginning of the winter and celebrate their "rebirth" at Easter time. Their members work either full time or part time as delivery boys and girls, unskilled workers, or in movie theaters. Their organizations charge membership dues and levy fines, and they receive additional revenue through public events. Once in a while they also commit petty theft. These teenagers feel closely connected through a strong feeling of solidarity and loving devotion to their organizations. They lead a somewhat rowdy and senseless life. In the present conditions of deprivation of proletarian youth, their existence would not be particularly worth mentioning if it were not for the fact that the hiking clubs are the chief source of recruits for the criminal gangs.

"Criminal gangs" is the name given to youth groups composed mainly of those who are depraved beyond help. These unhappy individuals were "expelled" from the normal process of personality development in early childhood due to grave errors in their education, severe traumas, and, most of all, unbearable deprivation. As a consequence, they never mastered the vital ability to adapt to social reality. In order to avoid depression and suicide, these gravely mistreated boys and girls create their own fantasy world as a compensation for the deprived existence they are forced to lead. It is a world with different norms, full of infantile and uninhibited drives, a world of hatred against the society that left them alone in pain and anguish.

---

6. "Die Cliquen jugendlicher Verwahrloster als sozialpädagogisches Problem," in *Sozial-pädagogische Schriftenreihe* (Potsdam: Alfred Protte Verlag); "Cliquenwesen und Jugendver-wahrlosung," *Zentralblatt für Jugendrecht und Jugendwohlfahrt*, March 1930 (Berlin: C. Heymanns Verlag).

The more harshly parents, educators, and judges treat them, the further they are driven into fantasy, into asocial and criminal behavior.

These neglected groups are most peculiar; peculiar in their mode of organization, but even more so in their rites. Their names reveal much about the gangs' character: Blood of the Tartars, Blood of the Trappers, Blood of the Indians, Blood of the Cossacks, Blood of the Gypsies, Gypsy Love, Wild Sow, Girl-Shy, Wild West, Peasant Scare, Red Apaches, Black Love, Red Oath, Fear Not Death, Bloody Bones, Dirty Guys, Forest and Field Sleepers, Tortoises, Brandy Thrush, Black Flag, Forest Pirates, Santa Fe, Northern Lights.[7] The atmosphere of these groups is strongly influenced by the stories of Karl May, by contempt for society and sentimental feelings, and by lack of inhibition. That they unabashedly pursue the satisfaction of their instincts is self-evident simply through their names.

When I heard that such teenagers could be found in Berlin's homosexual bars, I decided to conduct a field study and struck it lucky. A sparsely lit, small room, heavily filled with smoke, its ceiling drooping with paper garlands and oversized cardboard grapes, its walls adorned with kitschy classical landscapes, with tables set in paper arbors; in the center, bald-headed, potbellied petit bourgeois danced with boys dressed in sailor uniforms to the music of an old piano player: that's the Adonis Bar. By chance a nineteen-year-old "sailor," already a little tipsy, sat down at our table and told us the following.

Approximately four years ago, the wild gangs—my informer called them wild "guilds"—decided to organize themselves district by district into a "ring organization." Now there exist south, east, west, and north rings, a northeast ring, and so on. The leader of such a ring is called a "ring bull." The leader of a gang is called a "gang bull." An assembly of gang bulls elects the ring bull. To become a bull one must have a record of achievement and a diploma of success in diverse criminal activities, and proven mastery of the whole range of sexual activity. Courage and physical strength are the most important prerequisites. As some of these gangs discourage sexual contact with girls, girls increasingly form their own gangs, but they seldom

---

7. Tartarenblut, Trapperblut, Indianerblut, Kosakenblut, Zigeunerblut, Zigeunerliebe, Wildsau, Mädchenscheu, Wildwest, Bauernschreck, Rote Apachen, Schwarze Liebe, Roter Schwur, Todesverächter, Blutiger Knochen, Dreckstiebel, Wald- und Wiesenpenner, Schildkröte, Schnapsdrossel, Schwarzflaggen, Waldpiraten, Santa Fé, Nordlicht.

keep their independence very long. Over all, as many boys as girls join these gangs, and neither sex is in any way monogamous. In most cases the bull has a special "queen" just for him, but it also happens that a male gang has a "beloved" who is expected to be available to everyone. Almost every member carries an edelweiss as a symbol. Many gangs also dress in a characteristic way, a substitute for the uniform they would like to wear; for example, in traditional Tyrolian clothes, or American trapper style. One gang, the Eagles of the Mountains, consists only of bulls. On the occasion of joint meetings, mainly in bars in the western part of the city, members dress up in evening dinner jackets with tails and top hats. The chairman carries a long wooden club. Men and women like to wear earrings, and many are tattooed, in some cases even on their genitals. The members—boys are called "wild guys," girls "gang cows"—have to contribute money on a regular basis. Out of this they pay fines and support comrades hiding from the police. There are also apprentices to whom full membership is granted only after they have gone through a rather strange "baptism." In its sadism, this baptism resembles the very arduous initiation rites of primitive tribes or medieval guilds. Siegfried Bernfeld precisely shows this parallel in his book *The Community Life of Teenagers*.[8]

On the occasion of such a baptism, friendly gangs always meet in a deserted place, usually near one of Berlin's much beloved lakes such as the Lehnitzsee. The hiking gangs complete their initiation after a well-executed boxing match or a brawl with knives, or after the bull has thrown the new member completely dressed into the water. Criminal gangs expect their new members to fulfill some bizarre task such as completing sexual intercourse before the group in a specified time while the gang bull times the act with a stopwatch, or masturbating in front of an audience; to make a long story short, they perform exhibitionist activities. Very often the initiates have to strip, then are chained and smeared with excrement and urine. I won't even mention the baptismal meal the initiates have to eat!

These are not fairy tales—I myself saw pictures of such celebrations. Those early childhood drives, long forgotten by normal teenagers and transformed into other forms of eroticism, come to life again among these neglected juveniles as a consequence of their mental disturbances. The unconscious becomes reality.

8. *Vom Gemeinschaftsleben der Jugend.*

For the boys, the gangs provide comradeship, recognition, sexual satisfaction, and the attraction of danger and adventure. They are psychologically ready for such a life. Many of them find shelter in attics, cellars, and storage rooms, which are mainly furnished with cheap paperbacks and so-called *Stoszsofas,* or "fucking sofas." If they are unable to find shelter, they must sleep in employment offices or cinemas. During the parts of the day and night when they are not "going about their business," they generally huddle together in bars. These bars are special. This is best explained by noting that the gangs are closely connected with powerful organizations of pimps, for instance with Immertreu[9] in the Schlesicher Bahnhof.[10] It is not always easy to establish these links because organized pimps very often resist unorganized newcomers, leading to many bloody fights. These criminal gangs are a pre-school for organized crime and function as the army reserve of the underworld. In 1927–28, many bars sprang like mushrooms from the soil of Berlin. They functioned as meeting places and message centers, and also helped the gangs out of their difficult economic situation. Many of these bars are in the vicinity of Gormann and Münz streets. The gangs receive economic help from an innkeeper who grants the boys and girls loans of food and alcohol in exchange for their working papers or stolen valuables; or else, the innkeeper sells working papers to them in exchange for valuables. In either case the teenagers are in danger of clashing with their parents or the police.

To avoid this danger the young men go more and more into debt to the innkeeper and slide deeper and deeper into the underworld. The innkeeper is himself closely associated with the gangs and major criminal organizations and pays an insurance premium in the form of a high membership fee. This secures him regular customers who also function as his private police and protect him from unwelcome customers and the official police. In the sleazy bars of the Friedrichstrasse, not only the regular guests but even the doormen and waiters belong to the gang of pimps. If an innkeeper decides to fire a dancer without the agreement of such an organization, it might happen that his employees, whether he belongs to a gang or not, immediately go on strike. The whole mechanism works very well. To illustrate the lives and doings of these people, I want to quote from the letter of a gang member who happens to be an "automobile specialist."

9. "Forever Faithful."
10. One of the main railroad stations of Berlin.

A little later [I] managed to escape with H. Monday morning, I met the six of them sitting in an automobile close to the courthouse. I joined them. Soon we ran out of gas. We left the car where it was and went to the Friedrichstrasse. Here, "Auto"-Karl and M. took an Opel. We joined them in a side street. We drove to the Kurfürstendam[11] and switched from the Opel to another car. Then we drove through Struvenshof, Spandau, and Potsdam. We left the car in Schöneberg and took a Mercedes on the Kurfürstendam. We took the same car in the evening to the forest, where we spent the night. Tuesday morning we returned to Berlin. To get some money, we decided to unscrew some public telephones. All in all we took apart two telephones and made approximately 14 marks. The third attempt, near the Turnstrasse, failed. Afterward we drove to a canal near the Postsdam Bridge and threw the telephones into the water. Then we drove to a restaurant in Wedding.[12] After breakfast we had an accident involving a biker. We got out of the car in a hurry. "Auto"-Karl escaped with the car. I then met "Auto"-Karl at noon again in Schöneberg. He didn't want to stay with the others. Then we saw an Opel parked on the Hauptstrasse. We tried to break in, but the owner surprised us and we fled.

Those are the conditions under which thousands of youths in the big cities live. Here they are trained to become perfect criminals, here they acquire their ideals, and they in turn attract thousands of other children to a life of crime. They end up surrounded by high, thick walls, forever separated from normal life. What can be done? Which means could help prepare them for lives of dignity? How can we integrate them into society? Surely these questions are only too obvious. But I ask another question that must follow from these: Even if there is successful rehabilitation, what then?

Let us assume we had better schools, and that by prohibiting corporal punishment and introducing modern educational methods we would embitter our children less. Instead of hampering them, we would be promoting their natural development. Let us assume that in this way school had beneficial effects. Let us assume that the schools for delinquents were

11. Berlin's elegant shopping and café avenue.
12. A working-class district of Berlin.

improved and that the principals of these institutions understood something about student government, knew how to deal with the natural reactions of neglected teenagers, and were able to make them appreciate the institution instead of using methods that caused them to break out over and over again . . .

At this point I want to briefly mention the question of government funding. A welfare officer (Ehrhardt) has calculated the costs to the public fiscal budget. Fifty criminal delinquents committed 158 crimes and escaped 448 times from their correctional institutes. Twelve of them escaped more than once, 14 more than three times, 14 more than five times, 8 more than ten times, 5 more than fifteen times, and 6 more than twenty times. The lengths of their stay in schools for delinquents varied among the 50 cases: 2 stayed longer than half a year, 3 for more than a year, 4 for a year and a half, 7 for more than two years, 11 for more than three years, 16 for more than five years, and 7 for more than eight years. One day in a correctional institute costs RM 6. These 50 boys cost the public RM 422,570. The estimated cost of a simple escape is RM 20, for a total of RM 8,960. If we estimate that each criminal offense produces damages of about RM 100, this comes to RM 15,800, not counting the smaller offenses. We can conservatively estimate that the national economy suffered losses of RM 450,000. If we further remember that there are more than 200 inmates in Berlin alone, the estimated cost goes up to RM 1.75 million just for Berlin! These figures illustrate the insanity and failure of the system.

To return to the previous questions: If we assume that a sensible educational system would either prevent or remedy juvenile delinquency, what happens then? Reintegrated, probably educated as a craftsman, this boy is thrust into life as it exists today. Can he make it? Will he find a job? Where can he live? Where can he find even the minimum of happiness without which no one can bear to live in this world? I am afraid there is no answer to these questions. Perhaps only one solution is possible: A SOCIALIST EDUCATION THAT EQUIPS PROLETARIAN YOUTH TO STRUGGLE AGAINST THE CONDITIONS IN WHICH THEY FIND THEMSELVES!

Translation by Thomas Cassirer

GLOSSARY

Abbreviations

ADGB   Allgemeiner Deutscher Gewerkschaftsbund (General German Trade Union Federation; Socialist).

CGT   Confédération Général du Travail (General Labor Confederation). Today, this French trade union central is closely allied to the French Communist party, but during the period discussed in *La Peste brune* it was loyal to the Socialist International. Counterpart of the German ADGB.

DAF   Deutsche Arbeitsfront (German Labor Front).

Gestapo   Geheime Staatspolizei (Secret State Police).

KPD   Kommunistische Partei Deutschlands (Communist Party of Germany).

NSBO   Nationalsozialistische Betriebzellenorganisation (National Socialist Works Cells Organization).

NSDAP   Nationalsozialistische Deutsche Arbeiterpartei (National Socialist German Workers' party; Nazi party).

SA   Sturmabteilungen (lit., storm sections; i.e., Storm Troopers or "Brownshirts").

SAJ   Sozialistische Arbeiterjügend (Young Socialist Workers).

SAP   Sozialistische Arbeiterpartei (Socialist Workers' party; a left-wing splinter group of the Social Democrats).

Schupo   Die Schutzpolizei (constables).

SFIO   Section française de l'Internationale ouvrière (French Socialists led by Léon Blum).

SPD   Sozialdemokratische Partei Deutschlands (Social Democratic Party of Germany).

SS   Schutzstaffeln of the NSDAP (lit., protective echelons; the most powerful of the Nazi organizations).

Proper Names

AIMARD, OLIVIER GOUX [Gustave] (1818–1883). French author of exoticist adventure novels inspired by his travels; e.g., *Le Trappeur de l'Arkansas* (1853) and *Les Bandits de l'Arizona* (1882).

BEBEL, AUGUST (1840–1913). From 1865, chairman of the Workers' Educational Association of Leipzig, where he met Wilhelm Liebknecht. From 1869 on, he was the uncontested leader of the German Social Democratic party. A prolific writer, he also lived to see the Social Democrats become the largest party in the Reichstag (1912).

BLUM, LÉON (1872–1950). Collaborated with Jaurès on the socialist newspaper *l'Humanité*. At the Tours Congress (1920), was part of the Socialist minority that remained loyal to the Second (Socialist) International; became leader of the SFIO (French section of the Second International) and founded the newspaper *le Populaire*. Presided over the first Popular Front government from June 1936 to June 1937. In 1940 Blum was arrested by the Vichy regime, imprisoned, tried, and deported to Buchenwald and Dachau. After the war, he served briefly as premier once more in December 1946 and January 1947.

BRECHT, BERTOLT (1898–1956). Well-known German playwright and poet. He emigrated with his wife, the actress Helene Weigel, via Prague, Vienna, Switzerland, and Paris, to Denmark in 1933. He proceeded to Sweden in 1939, then in 1940 to Finland, and in 1941 via Moscow to the United States. Returned to Germany (GDR) after being subpoenaed by the House Committee on Un-American Activities during the McCarthy period.

DAUDET, ALPHONSE (1840–1897). French novelist who wrote, inter alia, the Tartarin burlesques in which the hero "is a genial caricature of the Frenchman of the Midi, a type proverbially mercurial and exuberant, boastful, but so carried away by his own tall stories that he believes them" (*Oxford Companion to French Literature*, 696).

DUDOW, SLATAN (1903–1963). Bulgarian-born German film producer known especially for his second film, *Kuhle Wampe* (1932). When Hitler took power, he went into exile and subsequently worked in the USSR and the GDR.

FRICK, WILHELM (1877–1946). Studied law and became director of the Bavarian political police in 1919. In January 1930, he became the first Nazi in a state government when he was named interior and education minister of Thuringia. In Hitler's first cabinet he served as Reich interior minister from 1933 to 1943. He played an important role in formulating the Civil Service Law of April 1933 and the Nuremberg race laws, as well as the concentration camp regime. At the Nuremberg trials in 1946, he was convicted of crimes against humanity, sentenced to death, and hanged.

GOEBBELS, JOSEPH (1897–1945). Joined the Nazi party in 1922, became Gauleiter of Berlin in 1926, and a Reichstag deputy in 1928. On May 14, 1933, he was named head of the new Ministry of Propaganda. Although Hitler had designated him as his successor, Goebbels committed suicide shortly after the Führer did.

GÖRING, HERMANN (1893–1946). Joined the Nazi party in 1922 and became the first leader of the SA. Elected a Reichstag deputy in 1928 and its president in 1932. Reich minister without portfolio, Reich air commissioner, and acting Prussian minister of the interior in Hitler's first cabinet. Committed suicide while awaiting execution at Nuremberg.

HINDENBURG, PAUL VON (1847–1934). German general and statesman. Named field marshal, 1914; elected second president of the Republic, 1925; appointed Hitler chancellor on January 30, 1933.

HITLER, ADOLF (1889–1945). Führer of the National Socialist movement. Of Austrian birth, he settled in Vienna where he became a building painter. Moved to Munich in 1913, served in World War I, and was employed by the Reichswehr as an agent against the revolutionary Left after the November 1918 revolution. Wrote *Mein Kampf* while in prison after the abortive Munich putsch of 1923. In elections for Reichspräsident in 1932, he obtained 36.8 percent of the vote, second only to Hindenburg, who named him chancellor on January 30, 1933.

JOUHAUX, LÉON (1879–1954). French syndicalist who joined the secretariat of the CGT in 1909. Arrested and deported to Germany in 1942, he returned to France in 1945 and was confederal secretary of the CGT until 1947. He then became secretary general of the newly founded splinter from the CGT, the CGT-FO (Force ouvrière).

LEIPART, THEODOR (1867–1947). A turner by vocation, he became president of the ADGB in 1920. Initially supported Chancellor Kurt von Schleicher's "economic stimulus" measures, which included overriding existing collective agreements. He was eventually persuaded by the SPD leadership to withdraw this support. Imprisoned by the Nazis after the "coordination" of the trade unions on May 2, 1933. In 1946, he joined the Socialist Unity party (SEP), which would become the governing party of the German Democratic Republic (DDR).

LEY, ROBERT (1890–1945). Succeeded Gregor Strasser as leader of the political organization of the Nazi party in 1932. Leader of the German Labor Front (DAF) 1933–1945. Played a leading role in the destruction of the trade unions. Committed suicide while awaiting trial at Nuremberg.

LIEBKNECHT, KARL (1871–1919). As a leftist Reichstag deputy of the German Social Democratic party, Liebknecht was sentenced to a prison term for his opposition to the First World War. After being pardoned in 1918 he joined Rosa Luxemburg as a leader of the Spartakist League, proclaiming the "Free Socialist Republic" on November 9, 1918, and organizing the Spartakist uprising in Berlin in January 1919. Arrested and murdered while being transferred to prison.

LIEBKNECHT, WILHELM (1826–1900). Socialist leader; helped to found the German Social Democratic Party. In May 1875, drafted the Gotha Program. He was editor in chief of the Social Democratic newspaper, *Vorwärts,* and served as Speaker of the Reichstag.

LUXEMBURG, ROSA (1870–1919). Polish-born German Socialist agitator and major Marxist theorist who dissociated herself from many of Lenin's more centralist and vanguardist positions. Leader, with Karl Liebknecht, of the Spartakist League and its insurrection in 1919. Arrested and murdered on January 15, 1919.

MAY, KARL (1842–1912). An immensely popular German adventure writer whose hero, the Teutonic knight Old Shatterhand, often confronted desperados on the North American plains.

PAPEN, FRANZ VON (1879–1969). German diplomat, soldier, and statesman. Chancellor from June to December 1932. He was briefly succeeded by Schleicher, whose government he helped bring down. Then he entered Hitler's government as vice chancellor.

PAUL-BONCOUR, JOSEPH. A French politician who served as minister of labor from 1911 to 1914. He cofounded the Union socialiste et républicaine and led it for many years. He quit the Socialist party (SFIO) in 1931 when he was elected a senator. His brief forty-day term as premier in one of a series of short-lived radical governments, coincided with Hitler's coming to power in Germany. Following France's capitulation to Germany in 1940, he was one of a minority of deputies to vote against the series of laws that established the Vichy regime.

RÖHM, ERNST (1887–1934). At the conclusion of the First World War, Röhm joined the Free Corps and participated in putting down the Munich "Republic of Councils" in 1919. Known for his penchant for extralegal tactics, he molded the SA into an instrument of violence and was named its chief of staff in 1930. After Hitler seized power, Röhm demanded that the SA be recognized as a national army. Hitler refused to do so and had Röhm and other SA leaders murdered on the Night of the Long Knives, at once removing his major rival within the party and placating the indignant Reichswehr.

SCHEIDEMANN, PHILIPP (1865–1939). Social Democratic politician. As people's commissioner, he proclaimed the Republic following the abdication of the Kaiser and was elected its first prime minister.

SCHLEICHER, KURT VON (1882–1934). German soldier and statesman. Helped bring about the collapse of the Brüning government in May 1932; appointed Reichswehr minister in the succeeding Papen cabinet; served as chancellor from December 1932 to January 1933. Murdered by the SS on June 30, 1934.

STRASSER, GREGOR (1892–1934). A pharmacist by training, Strasser became a Nazi in 1921 and was a Reichstag deputy for the Nazi party from 1924 to 1932. In 1926, he founded Kampf Verlag, which published his "left-Nazi" views. He called for the nationalization of banks and heavy industry, criticized the Weimar system, and railed against the twin evils of capitalism and communism while calling for an organic, *Volkisch* community. He was Reich propaganda leader from 1926 until he was replaced by Joseph Goebbels in 1930. He was murdered on the Night of the Long Knives.

THÄLMANN, ERNST [Teddy] (1886–1944). Leading Communist politician and Reichstag deputy. A longshoreman and transport worker, Thälmann joined the KPD in 1920 and became its party chairman in Hamburg in 1921. In 1925, he became chairman of the KPD and from that time until 1932 ran regularly as the Communist candidate for president. Arrested after the Reichstag fire, he was imprisoned for the following eleven years until he was murdered at Buchenwald concentration camp.

WESSEL, HORST (1907–1930). A student who joined the Nazis in 1926 and the SA shortly thereafter in the Berlin district of Friedrichshain. He was shot in the mouth during a brawl that started after a pimp, jealous of Wessel's romantic involvement with one of his prostitutes, led a group of Red Front militants to him. A poem written by Wessel was set to a sailor's march, "Die Fahnehoch," and made the second national anthem after 1933. Wessel himself became revered as a martyr to the Nazi movement.

Becker, Howard. *German Youth: Bond or Free.* London: Kegan Paul, Trench, Trubner, 1946.

Berstein, Serge. *La France des années 1930.* Paris: Armand Colin Editeur, 1988.

Bracher, Karl Dietrich. *The German Dictatorship: The Origins, Structure, and Effects of National Socialism.* Trans. Jean Steinber. New York: Praeger, 1970.

———. "Stages of Totalitarian 'Integration' (*Gleichschaltung*): The Consolidation of National Socialist Rule in 1933 and 1934." In *Republic to Reich,* ed. Hajo Holborn, pp. 109–28.

Brasillach, Robert. *Une Génération dans l'orage. Mémoires. Notre avant-guerre* et *Journal d'un homme occupé.* Paris: Plon, 1968.

The Brown Book of the Hitler Terror and the Burning of the Reichstag, by the World Committee for the Victims of German Fascism. London: Victor Gollancz, 1933.

Buchheim, Hans. "The Position of the SS in the Third Reich." In *Republic to Reich,* ed. Hajo Holborn, pp. 251–97.

Chadbourne, Ellis. *Youth's Crusade. The Meaning of the Youth Movement.* Fairfield, Conn.: Youth Publications, 1928.

Dictionary of German History 1806–1945, by Wildried Fest. New York: St. Martin's Press, 1978.

Dictionnaire de la politique française, dir. Henry Coston. Paris: Henry Coston, 1967.

Encyclopedia of the Third Reich, by Louis L. Snyder. New York: McGraw-Hill, 1976. [*ETR*]

The Encyclopedia of the Third Reich, by Christian Zentner and Friedmann Bedürftig. 2 vols. New York: Macmillan, 1991. [*ETR,* 1991]

France 1789–1962, by James J. Cooke. Hamden, Conn.: Archon Books, 1975.

Ginzburg, Carlo. "Germanic Mythology and Nazism: Thoughts on an Old Book by Georges Dumézil." In *Clues, Myths, and the Historical Method,* trans. John and Anne C. Tedeschi, pp. 126–45. Baltimore: Johns Hopkins University Press, 1989.

Le Grand Robert des noms propres. Paris: Le Robert, 1986.

Guérin, Daniel. *Autobiographie de jeunesse: d'une dissidence sexuelle au socialisme.* Paris: Pierre Belfond, 1971.

———. *Le feu du sang. Autobiographie politique et charnelle.* Paris: Grasset, 1977.

———. *Son Testament.* Paris: Encres, 1979.

Bibliography

Heiden, Konrad. *Der Fuehrer: Hitler's Rise to Power*. Trans. Ralph Manheim. Boston: Houghton Mifflin, 1944.

Holborn, Hajo, ed. *Republic to Reich: The Making of the Nazi Revolution. Ten Essays*. Trans. Ralph Manheim. New York: Pantheon Books, 1972.

"Homosexuality and Male Bonding in Pre-Nazi Germany." Ed. Harry Oosterhuis. Special issue of *Journal of Homosexuality* 22 (1991): 1–2.

Isherwood, Christopher. *Christopher and His Kind 1929–1939*. London: Eyre Methuen, 1976.

———. *Mr. Norris Changes Trains* and *Goodbye to Berlin* (1939). Reprint. Introduction by James Fenton. London: Chatto and Windus, 1985.

Krausnick, Helmut, Hans Buchheim, Martin Broszat, and Hans-Adolf Jacobsen. *Anatomy of the SS State*. Trans. Richard Barry et al. London: Collins, 1968.

Laqueur, Walter. *Young Germany: A History of the German Youth Movement*. New Brunswick, N.J.: Transaction Books, 1984.

Mann, Erika. *School for Barbarians: Education under the Nazis*. London: Lindsay Drummon, 1939.

Mann, Heinrich. *Berlin*. 1900. Reprint. London: Victor Gollancz, 1929.

Mann, Klaus. *The Pious Dance*. 1925. Reprint. New York: FAJ, 1987.

———. *The Turning Point*. New York: Fischer, 1942.

Mann, Thomas. *Diaries 1918–1939*. New York: Abrams, 1982.

———. *Letters of Thomas Mann 1889–1955*. New York: Knopf, 1971.

Matthias, Erich. "The Downfall of the Old Social Democratic Party in 1933." In *Republic to Reich*, ed. Hajo Holborn, pp. 51–105.

Mommsen, Hans. "The Reichstag Fire and Its Political Consequences." In *Republic to Reich*, ed. Hajo Holborn, pp. 129–222.

Mosse, George L. *Nazi Culture: Intellectual, Cultural, and Social Life in the Third Reich*. Trans. Salvator Attanasio et al. New York: Grosset and Dunlap, 1966.

Noakes, Jeremy, and Geoffrey Pridham, eds. *Documents on Nazism 1919–1945*. London: Jonathan Cape, 1974.

———. *Nazism 1919–1945. A History in Documents and Eyewitness Accounts*. Vol. 1: *The Nazi Party, State, and Society 1919–1939*. New York: Schocken Books, 1983.

The Oxford Companion to French Literature, by Harvey and Heseltine. Oxford: Oxford University Press, 1959.

The Oxford Companion to German Literature, by Mary Garland. 2d ed. Oxford: Oxford University Press, 1986.

Peukert, Detlev J. K. *Inside Nazi Germany: Conformity, Opposition, and Racism in Everyday Life*. New Haven: Yale University Press, 1987.

Proctor, Robert. *Racial Hygiene. Medicine under the Nazis*. Cambridge: Harvard University Press, 1988.

Schleunes, Karl A. *The Twisted Road to Auschwitz: Nazi Policy Toward German Jews 1933–1939*. Urbana: University of Illinois Press, 1970.

Spender, Stephen. Introduction to *Herbert List Photographs 1930–1970*. New York: Rizzoli, 1980.

———. Introduction to *Herbert List: Junge Männer* (photographs). Altadena, Calif.: Twin Palms, 1988.

———. *The Temple.* London: Faber and Faber, 1988.

———. *World Within World.* London: Hamish Hamilton, 1951.

Steakley, James D. *The Homosexual Emancipation Movement in Germany.* New York: Arno Press, 1975.

Stern, Fritz. *Dreams and Delusions: National Socialism and the Drama of the German Past.* New York: Vintage Books, 1989.

Wescott, Glenway. *Fear and Trembling.* New York: Harper and Brothers, 1932.

Weygand, le Général. *Comment élever nos fils?* Paris: Flammarion, 1937.

Who's Who in Nazi Germany, by Robert Wistrich. New York: Macmillan, 1982.

Wormser-Migot, Olga. *Le Système concentrationnaire nazi (1933–1945).* Paris: Presses universitaires de France, 1968.

INDEX

AIZ (Arbeiter Illustrierte Zeitung), 66, 107

Anti-Nazi resistance, 1, 33–35; clandestine and illegal activities, 2, 34, 79, 134–36, 143, 146–47, 150–52, 161; Communists and, 71, 132–33, 153–57; defense groups, 19, 108, 144–45; intellectuals and, 29–30; international solidarity, 82; internment of resistors, 28–29; "noncompliance" versus resistance, 34–35; Socialists and, 71, 135, 142–47; Trotskyists and, 156; workers in Hamburg, 148–49; women and, 151; youth and, 146–47, 153–54

Anti-Semitism, 2, 21, 30–33, 106, 109–13, 139, 159; in France, 8–11; *Jews Are Watching You*, 111–12; songs, 121–22

"Aryans," 33, 101, 109–11. *See also* "Racial purity"

Auden, W. H., 13

Barr, Arno, 82–83

Blum, Léon, 8, 73, 79

Bolshevism, 91, 103, 120. *See also* Communist International; Lenin; Stalin; Trotsky; U.S.S.R.

Book burnings, 2, 14, 105–8, 139, 143

Bracher, Karl Dietrich, 24

Brasillach, Robert, 10–11

Brecht, Bertolt, 2, 68, 75

"Bringing into conformity." *See Gleichschaltung*

Brown Houses. *See* Nazi Party

Brownshirts. *See* Storm Troopers

Brüning, Heinrich, 18

Capitalism: crisis of, 110; fascism and, 7, 162–63; nationalism and, 155; Nazism and, 60, 83, 120–21, 161

Children: *Amis de l'enfance ouvrière*, 112, 135, 145–46; anti-Nazi resistance and, 151–52; Nazis and, 35, 55, 85, 96, 134, 148, 161; schoolchildren, 50, 115; social reform and, 171–72

Communist International, 153–55, 157. *See also* Communist Party of Germany

Communist Party of France (PCF), 8, 81–82; *l'Humanité*, 81

Communist Party of Germany (KPD), 81; attitude toward Social Democratic Party, 20, 58–59, 70–73; Communist International and, 71–72, 154–55; founding of, 23; internal opposition and, 156–57; at Kuhle Wampe, 69; Nazi terror against, 24–25, 137–39; parliamentary caucus, 63; party strategy and tactics, 20, 70, 153–56; propaganda, press, and publications, 55, 107–8; in "Red" neighborhoods, 69–70, 75–76, 138, 149, 154, 161; *Rote Fahne*, 50, 152, 156; trade unions and, 58, 124–26; youth and, 56, 70, 153–54, 166. *See also* Anti-Nazi resistance

Concentration camps. *See* Repression

Conservative Party (Germany): parliamentary caucus, 63

"Coordination." *See Gleichschaltung*

DAF. *See* German Labor Front

Dudow, Slatan, 2, 68

Daniel Guérin was an independent French leftist intellectual and the author of more than forty works on topics including anarchism, homosexuality, decolonization, and the French Revolution. He died in 1988. Robert Schwartzwald is Associate Professor of French at the University of Massachusetts at Amherst.

Library of Congress Cataloging-in-Publication Data
Guérin, Daniel, 1904–
[Peste brune. English]
The brown plague : travels in late Weimar and early Nazi Germany / Daniel Guérin ; translated and with an introduction by Robert Schwartzwald.
Includes bibliographical references.
ISBN 0-8223-1457-6 (alk. paper). —
ISBN 0-8223-1463-0 (pbk. : alk. paper)
1. Germany—Politics and government—1918–1933.
2. Germany—Politics and government—1933–1945.
3. National socialism—Germany.   4. Political culture—Germany—History—20th century.   I. Title.
DD240.G79 1994
943.085—dc20   93-48481 CIP